experience and a passion for travel.

**Rely on Thomas Cook as your
travelling companion on your next trip
and benefit from our unique heritage.**

Thomas Cook **pocket** guides

BRUGES
Anwer Bati

Written and updated by Anwer Bati

Published by Thomas Cook Publishing
A division of Thomas Cook Tour Operations Limited
Company registration no. 3772199 England
The Thomas Cook Business Park, Unit 9, Coningsby Road,
Peterborough PE3 8SB, United Kingdom
Email: books@thomascook.com, Tel: +44 (0) 1733 416477
www.thomascookpublishing.com

Produced by Cambridge Publishing Management Limited
Burr Elm Court, Main Street, Caldecote CB23 7NU
www.cambridgepm.co.uk

ISBN: 978-1-84848-536-5

© 2006, 2008, 2010 Thomas Cook Publishing
This fourth edition © 2012 Thomas Cook Publishing
Text © Thomas Cook Publishing
Maps © Thomas Cook Publishing/PCGraphics (UK) Limited
Transport map © Communicarta Limited

Series Editor: Karen Beaulah
Production/DTP: Steven Collins

Printed and bound in Spain by GraphyCems

Cover photography © Danita Delimont/Alamy

All rights reserved. No part of this publication may be reproduced, stored in
a retrieval system or transmitted, in any form or by any means, electronic,
mechanical, recording or otherwise, in any part of the world, without prior
permission of the publisher. Requests for permission should be made to the
publisher at the above address.

Although every care has been taken in compiling this publication, and the contents
are believed to be correct at the time of printing, Thomas Cook Tour Operations
Limited cannot accept any responsibility for errors or omissions, however caused,
or for changes in details given in the guidebook, or for the consequences of any
reliance on the information provided. Descriptions and assessments are based on
the author's views and experiences when writing and do not necessarily represent
those of Thomas Cook Tour Operations Limited.

CONTENTS

POCKET GUIDES

SYMBOLS KEY
The following symbols are used throughout this book:

🅐 address 🅣 telephone 🅦 website address 🅛 opening times
🅝 public transport connections 🅘 important

The following symbols are used on the maps:

🄸 information office   ▪ point of interest
🛪 airport
➕ hospital
🄲 police station
🚌 bus station
🚆 railway station
✝ cathedral
❶ numbers denote featured
   cafés & restaurants

Hotels and restaurants are graded by approximate price as follows:
£ budget price ££ mid-range price £££ expensive

❶ Bruges oozes charm with its old buildings and canals

INTRODUCING
Bruges

Introduction

Bruges – Brugge in Dutch – is a city on a human scale. There are no high-rise buildings, no traffic-jammed boulevards or heavy industrial plants. Instead, look forward to cobbled streets, medieval architecture and, around every corner, a striking new vista to admire.

Thriving industry based around the port of Zeebrugge recalls the glory days of the 13th to 16th centuries, when Bruges was one of the most important ports in Europe and a lucrative centre of trade. These days, however, after years of meticulous reconstruction efforts on its precious buildings, it is mainly tourism that keeps the city's economy alive. Easy to access, safe to walk around with its large, pedestrianised areas, calm and quiet due to strict noise regulations, it is a gem of a city that retains a powerful aura of the past.

Bruges is a city of both high culture and good living. The entire historic centre was designated a UNESCO World Heritage Site in 2000 and is packed with impressive buildings and churches containing stunning examples of Flemish art of all eras. Music thrives in the huge Concertgebouw as well as other cosier venues throughout the city. Visitors join with the 117,000-strong population to celebrate festivals and large-scale historical events and traditions, particularly in the summer. The city may be small, but its attractions are growing every year.

When night falls you'll find restaurants and bars of all descriptions serving up tasty regional specialities, including the famous Belgian chips, along with a dizzying range of locally brewed beers and the trademark flavoured gin. There are no riotous neon-lit nightclubs in the city, but you can enjoy the simple pleasures of a cosy evening meal, a quiet drink in a bar, or a stroll through the beautiful lit-up buildings and along the canals. A night – and a city – to remember.

◆ *It's easy to find your way around in the centre*

When to go

High season stretches from Easter to September, with particularly busy patches in July and August. If you can choose when to visit and don't mind missing the warmth of spring and summer, however, it's best to go out of season to avoid the high prices and crowds. The Christmas market in Markt (see page 11) is one excellent reason to visit during the winter. Although Bruges is the perfect size for a long weekend, again you'll have a quieter holiday if you can come during the week – but note that most museums are closed on Monday.

SEASONS & CLIMATE

Belgium's climate is broadly similar to that of Britain. Temperatures range from average lows of 1°C (34°F) in winter to average highs of 21°C (70°F) in summer. Spring and autumn are both mild and pleasant. Winter, although rather rainy and foggy, doesn't usually bring much frost or snow.

ANNUAL EVENTS

There are lively festivals in Bruges all year round. The emphasis is increasingly on outdoor events, such as the lively two-week Klinkers Music Festival in July–August, and on events held outside of the usual high season, including the new December Dance Festival. Look out for small but fascinating temporary exhibitions held by leading museums including the Groeninge (see page 82).

March

Cinema Novo Festival Cinema festival focused on films made in developing countries. ⓐ Cinema Lumière & Ciné Liberty ⓦ www.cinemanovo.be

WHEN TO GO

April & May
Ronde van Vlaanderen (Tour of Flanders) (1st Sun in Apr) A 250-km (155-mile) international cycle race with around 250 competitors completing the course in just one day. The race starts in the Markt. ⓦ www.rondevanvlaanderen.be

🔺 *The Christmas fair is a good reason to visit in the winter*

Choco-Laté/Chocolate Market (late Apr–early May) The city-wide chocolate festival Choco-Laté, centred on Sint-Janshospitaal, now alternates with a chocolate market. The market (housed at the Belfort) is next held in 2012, with Choco-Laté in 2013. The latter includes competitions, a children's chocolate village, workshops and special chocolate dishes at restaurants around Bruges. Ⓦ www.choco-late.be

Melfoor (early May) Funfair held over three weeks at various locations: 't Zand; Hawerstraat; Beursplein; Simon Stevinplein; Koning Albertpark. There are usually fireworks on the opening evening.

Heiligbloedprocessie (Procession of the Holy Blood) (Ascension Day) See page 63. Ⓦ www.holyblood.com

July & August

Cactus Festival (2nd week in July) Open-air music festival featuring world music, rap and dance. Ⓦ www.cactusmusic.be

Nationale feestdag (Belgian National Holiday) (21 July) Colourful celebrations including bands and outdoor entertainment.

Musica Antiqua (Early Music Festival of Flanders) (late July–early Aug) Concerts of early classical music in various locations (see page 12). Ⓦ www.musica-antiqua.be

Klinkers (late July–Aug) Lively open-air music and film festival (see page 12). Ⓦ www.klinkers-brugge.be

Lace Days Two days of lace making demonstrations, stalls and street entertainment. Ⓦ www.kantcentrum.com

November

Brugges Festival Well-established three-day festival of world music and folk at the City Theatre and Biekorf Theatre. Ⓦ www.bruggesfestival.be

December
December Dance Festival (early Dec) New festival celebrating live music and dance around the city. Ⓦ www.concertgebouw.be
Kerstmarkt (Christmas Market) (late Nov–1 Jan) Festive market with craft and gift stalls, mulled wine and a temporary ice rink. ❸ Markt ❶ 050 44 46 46 🕐 Market: 11.00–19.30; ice rink: 12.00–21.00

PUBLIC HOLIDAYS
Nieuwjaarsdag (New Year's Day) 1 Jan
Pasen & Paasmaandag (Easter Sun & Mon) 8 & 9 Apr 2012, 31 Mar & 1 Apr 2013, 20 & 21 Apr 2014
Dag van de Arbeid (Labour Day) 1 May
OLH Hemelvaart (Ascension Day) 17 May 2012, 9 May 2013, 29 May 2014
Pinksteren & Pinkstermaandag (Whit Sun & Mon) 27 & 28 May 2012, 19 & 20 May 2013, 8 & 9 June 2014
Feest van de Vlaamse Gemeenschap (Flemish Community Holiday) 11 July
Nationale feestdag (Belgian National Holiday) 21 July
OLV Hemelvaart (Assumption) 15 Aug
Allerheiligen (All Saints' Day) 1 Nov
Wapenstilstand (Armistice Day) 11 Nov
Kerstmis (Christmas Day) 25 Dec

All banks and businesses and most shops, cafés and restaurants close on public holidays. If Sunday is a holiday, many places close on Monday as well, and if Thursday is a holiday, people take Friday off too.

City of festivals

Bruges is not just about historic buildings and quiet canal-side walks. Noise regulations in the centre mean that thumping nightclubs are thin on the ground, but come during one of Bruges's buzzing festivals and you'll see a very different side of town. Arrive the day of the notorious 'Benenwerk' (literally 'leg work') dance party, for example, and you'll find anything from waltz to break-dance, rave to hip hop, swing to salsa, on every street corner of the historic centre.

The Benenwerk is the culmination of the Klinkers Festival held over two weeks in July–August, an unmissable free open-air celebration of contemporary music, dance and film for which the city is becoming rightly famous. The organisers seek out raw, fresh talent and lure concert-hall musicians into the open to play in historic locations around the city. The Cactus Festival, a three-day world music festival in the Minnewaterpark staged prior to Klinkers by the same organisers, is a warm-up for the city-wide events.

Classical music gets its turn at the Musica Antiqua (Early Music) Festival and competition in July and August. Running annually for almost five decades as part of the regional Flanders Festival, it has established itself as one of the most prominent cultural events in the world.

Winter sees a bright spot with the international December Dance Festival, run in part by the Concertgebouw. Renowned dancers coordinate performances of live music and dance throughout the city during the first two weeks of December. Even if you're just watching, it's the perfect way to warm up on a frosty winter's day.

See page 8 for contact details and for listings of other festivals in Bruges.

⬤ 'Benenwerk' turns the historic centre into one enormous dance floor

History

The first references to the Municipium Brugense, or Bryggia, appeared in the 7th century. The name derives from Norse and means 'jetty' or 'landing place', a particularly apt description when the city – linked to the sea by the Zwin estuary – grew to become one of the most important ports in northwest Europe.

Under the patronage of the Counts of Flanders the city developed economically, becoming in 1309 the first city in the Low Countries to open a sophisticated money market. The van der Beurse family who ran it gave their name to the term that is used for stock exchanges around the world (*bourse*).

Bruges reached its commercial pinnacle in the 14th and 15th centuries with the production of woollen cloth and luxury goods. It began trading extensively around Europe, including with England and Scotland. Foreign merchants flocked to the city to set up trading houses and goods were imported from all over the world.

Economic prosperity went hand in hand with cultural activity. Under the Dukes of Burgundy from the end of the 14th century, Bruges became an artistic centre attracting great Flemish painters such as Jan van Eyck and Hans Memling. Fine buildings sprang up all over the city, increasing its status and power in the region.

Bruges's fortunes were inextricably linked to the sea – ships would moor at Markt to unload their goods – and the city suffered badly in the 16th century when the Zwin estuary finally silted up. With the formerly lucrative port cut off from the sea, the city's population's attempts at reviving their economy through improved maritime infrastructure and a new lace industry were not entirely successful. Bruges remained quiet for several centuries. The 19th-century Belgian poet Georges Rodenbach rather cruelly labelled the

city 'Bruges la Morte' (Dead Bruges) for its stagnant economy and mysterious atmosphere.

Ambitious projects in the early 20th century, including the building of the port of Zeebrugge and the cutting of a new canal, gave life back to the city, and it is now packed with tourists eager to admire its beautiful monuments, museums and historic houses. Most of these escaped largely unscathed from both world wars, although paradoxically, one of the most visited places in the area is the devastated town of Ypres with its sombre World War I battlefields and cemeteries.

Meticulous reconstruction works have restored many of the city's buildings to their former glory and the entire historic centre has been designated a UNESCO World Heritage Site. Visual and performing arts are thriving, and festivals celebrating both traditional and modern events draw tourists from all over the world. With this happy revival in both its culture and its economy, Bruges looks set to enjoy a long and prosperous future.

● *Bruges's city centre is a UNESCO World Heritage Site*

Lifestyle

Belgians enjoy a well-deserved reputation for openness and friendliness, and this is especially true in Bruges where tourism is a mainstay of the economy. The British are particularly welcomed, partly due to historic links involving the wool trade and partly because it was the influx of British visitors in the 19th century that encouraged the restoration of the city centre. Expect a friendly welcome and a helpful attitude from inhabitants in return for your respect towards them and their city.

FLANDERS, FLEMISH, DUTCH & FRENCH

The two largest regions in Belgium are the Dutch-speaking Flanders in the north, containing almost two-thirds of the population, and the French-speaking Wallonia in the south, containing just under a third. The small remaining fraction live in and around Brussels in the bilingual Brussels-Capital region, and there is a small German community in Wallonia.

Bruges is the capital of the West Flanders province and very proudly Flemish. Dutch is the first language, although you will often see French on menus, in hotels and in other publications. Many residents, especially older ones, also speak French, but most Flemings are just as likely to speak good English.

Look out for variations in place names. 'Bruges' is the French name for the Dutch 'Brugge'; 'Ghent' is 'Gand' in French and 'Gent' in Dutch, and 'Ypres' in Dutch is 'Ieper'. In this book, the names most familiar to English-speaking readers are used, with the alternatives in brackets.

● *Refreshment is never far away*

The standard of living in Belgium is generally high, but the cost of living has not yet caught up and you should find prices cheaper than in other popular destinations on the Continent. Tourism tends to drive prices up, so if you want to find a cheap meal and to eat or drink with locals, head away from the busy city centre around Markt.

The residents of Bruges are proud of their Flemish culture and fond of their city. They are also proud of their reputation for cuisine and beer-brewing, and love to have a good time. Food, drink, music, dance and festivals play a big part in the city's life and, for the most part, you'll find its people are more than happy to share it with you.

Culture

Art and culture were strong in Bruges as far back as the Middle Ages, and the cultural scene is no less active today. Residents of the city are keen to display its rich heritage to visitors, and there are numerous opportunities to visit museums, admire some impressive architecture and participate in lively local events and festivals. Simply wandering around with your eyes open, soaking up the atmosphere, can be a powerful experience, particularly in the areas around the attractive canals.

Museum fans should head for the Groeninge Museum (see page 82) with its fine collection of Flemish, Dutch and Belgian paintings, and also for the smaller Memling in Sint-Jan Hospitaalmuseum (see page 83). When you've exhausted these, visit the Arentshuis (see page 81) to see work by Frank Brangwyn, the early 20th-century British artist who was born in Bruges. The Gruuthuse Museum (see page 82) offers a glimpse of the life of a wealthy nobleman at a time when Bruges was at its commercial zenith.

BRUGGEMUSEUM

The whole of Bruges's city centre was designated a UNESCO World Heritage Site in 2000. Several buildings, however, enjoy a special status under the umbrella title *Bruggemuseum* (Bruges Museum). These include the Gruuthuse (see page 82), the Onze-Lieve-Vrouwekerk (Church of Our Lady, see page 78), the Archaeology Museum (see page 81), the Belfort (see page 63), the Stadhuis (Town Hall, see page 66) and the Paleis van het Brugse Vrije (Palace of Bruges Liberty, see page 66).

● *The Groeninge Museum has an excellent range of exhibits*

TICKETS & CULTURAL LISTINGS

If you're staying for a couple of days or more, it's well worth getting a **Brugge City Card**. This allows free admission to 22 museums and attractions, as well as a canal tour and various discounts. It is available online (Ⓦ www.bruggecitycard.be) or from the tourist offices at 't Zand and the station. You can buy cards for 48 hours or 72 hours, and a visitor's guide is included in the price.

Otherwise, you can buy tickets at the museums or the tourist office. To book for performances visit Ⓦ www.tickets brugge.be

Municipal museums offer concessions for people under 26 and over 60, and children under 13 can enter free. Be prepared for long queues in high season.

Exit (Ⓦ www.exit.be) is a free monthly Bruges listings magazine, available in the Town Hall, library and various bookshops and bars.

In Bruges itself, visit the **In&Uit Brugge** tourist office at the Concertgebouw (Ⓐ 't Zand 34 Ⓣ 050 44 86 86 Ⓦ www.brugge.be Ⓛ 10.00–18.00 Fri–Wed, 10.00–20.00 Thur).

For something more idiosyncratic try the Museum voor Volkskunde (Folklore Museum, see page 99), Choco-Story (see page 90) or the De Halve Maan Brewery (see page 78), the last remaining brewery in town. Remember that many museums are closed on Mondays.

For information on performing arts see page 31.

▶ *A ride in a horse-drawn carriage is a great way to see the city*

 # MAKING THE MOST OF
Bruges

Shopping

Bruges is packed to bursting with small, quirky shops selling everything from genuine antiques and lace to contemporary designer clothing. The city centre is thankfully free of big supermarkets and large department stores, leaving quality chain shops such as Zara and Mango to mingle with the privately run boutiques. You will also find outlets for several major Belgian luxury brands including Delvaux.

The main shopping street in Bruges is Steenstraat, just off Markt, leading on to Zuidzandstraat and 't Zand Square. The area known as Zilverpand, nestling between Zuidzandstraat and Noordzandstraat, contains a maze of arcades housing small boutiques.

Other major shopping streets are Geldmuntstraat and Vlamingstraat. On Wollestraat, which runs south of Markt along Belfort, you will find the well-known design shop Callebert (see page 68) and some quality lace shops that keep Bruges's tradition of lacemaking alive.

USEFUL SHOPPING PHRASES

How much is...?
Hoeveel kost (het)...?
Hoo-fayl kost (het)...?

I'm a size...
Ik heb maat...
Ik hep maat...

Can I try this on?
Mag ik dit passen?
Makh ik dit passen?

I'll take this one
Deze neem ik
Day-ze naym ik

🔺 *Look out for odd, quirky shops such as The Bear Necessities (see page 84)*

Hoogstraat has a number of antiques and interior shops, and St-Amandsstraat is good for jewellery and other luxury goods. For cheap and cheerful souvenirs and gifts head for Katelijnestraat and Mariastraat.

● *Bruges offers a wide variety of tempting chocolate treats*

CHOCOLATE

Chocolate in Belgium is not so much an edible treat as an art form. Bruges even has a museum dedicated to it (see page 90) and a festival to celebrate its production and use (see page 10). There are over 50 chocolate shops around town but only five of them make chocolate on the premises. They include **Sukerbuyc** (🅰 Katelijnestraat 5 📞 050 33 08 87 🌐 www.sukerbuyc.be), **Van Oost** (🅰 Wollestraat 11 📞 050 33 14 54 🌐 www.chocolatiervanoost.be) and **The Chocolate Line** (🅰 Simon Stevinplein 17 📞 050 34 10 90 🌐 www.thechocolate line.be), for a less traditional take on Belgian chocolate.

Quirky shops to look out for include **The Bear Necessities** (see page 84), which sells only teddy bears, and **De Striep** (🅰 Katelijnestraat 42 🌐 www.destriep.be), which offers a large selection of Belgian comic-strip (*bande desinée* or *stripverhalen*) books.

If the weather is fine, you may prefer the buzz of a local market to shopping indoors. Lively food and clothing markets are held at 08.00–13.00 in Markt on Wednesdays and at Beursplein and 't Zand Square on Saturdays. The weekend flea market along Dijver also opens on Fridays in July and August and, if the weather is good, stallholders stay until 18.00 to catch browsing tourists.

Food and drink shops abound in Bruges, with some excellent delicatessens selling local or French cheeses and other national specialities such as the wafer-thin *kletskoppen* biscuits. Try Deldycke delicatessen (see page 68), where the food is beautifully displayed. You should also pick up some local beer or *jenever* (gin), to sample here or take home.

Eating & drinking

Flemish cuisine has the heartiness and simplicity of Dutch cooking along with some continental twists reflecting the history of the area. French-influenced dishes appear on most menus and there are elements of Spanish cuisine in some local recipes.

Meat, particularly beef and game (when in season), is excellent and local fish and seafood (including oysters) are widely available. Most dishes are served with chips, which Belgians claim are the best in the world, partly due to the high quality of local potatoes and partly because the chips (*frietjes* in Dutch or *frites* in French) are fried twice. The quintessential Belgian dish of mussels and chips is served everywhere.

If the typically large portions haven't filled you up, you can also feast on the huge range of excellent biscuits and pastries available from local patisseries, as well as, of course, chocolate.

Restaurants are generally open 12.00–14.30 and 18.00–22.30 or 23.00, often later in high season, though kitchens are likely to close around 21.00–21.30. You will, though, find brasseries and cafés serving food throughout the day. Menus are normally printed in Dutch and French, and frequently in English as well. Smoking is

PRICE CATEGORIES
Restaurant ratings in this book are based on the average price of a three-course dinner without drinks. Lunchtime and set menus will often be cheaper.
£ up to €20   ££ €20–75   £££ over €75

LOCAL SPECIALITIES

For some traditional local food, scan the menu for *stoverij* (*carbonnades* in French), a rich, sweet dish of beef stewed in beer and usually served with *frietjes* (chips). For something lighter try *waterzooi*, a typical dish from Ghent originally consisting of fish and vegetables cooked in cream but now also made using chicken.

Belgian seafood specialities *maatjes* (raw herring), *mosselen* (mussels) and *paling* (eel) are best eaten in season. Eat *maatjes* in June, served with chopped raw onion and washed down with a shot of local *jenever* (gin). Mussels are eaten from September through to April, traditionally cooked in white wine, onions, celery and parsley.

Other specialities include *witloof* (endive) and ham gratin, *stoemp* (potatoes mashed together with vegetables), *garnaalkroketten* (deep-fried potato and shrimp croquettes), *hopscheuten* (hop shoots in cream) and *wafels* (hot, sugary waffles).

banned in restaurants but you can still light up outside. The total ban on smoking inside public places was imposed in 2011.

Restaurant prices are fairly high, partly due to Belgium's VAT of 21 per cent and partly because a hefty 16 per cent service charge is usually included in the bill. There is no need to tip extra unless you have been given particularly special treatment. To save money on restaurants, avoid the area immediately around Markt, go for a set menu at lunchtime, and ask for tap water over mineral water (many restaurants in tourist areas will refuse, however).

Eating alfresco along the canal or in parks such as Minnewater or Astridpark just south of Markt is pleasant, particularly in summer, and there are plenty of small bakeries, stalls and delicatessens from which to buy your picnic. The food markets (see page 25) are also a good bet for some lovely, fresh produce.

In terms of popular local drinks, you won't go wrong with beer or gin. Belgians use both regularly in cooking as well as enjoying them in bars. Gin is often flavoured and has an aromatic taste distinct from the bitterness of dry British gin. Beer-making has a long history in Belgium – particularly in the monasteries – and is taken very seriously. There are more than 600 Belgian beers, some flavoured with fruit and other infusions, and many bars dedicated to serving rare brands. 't Brugs Beertje (see page 88), for instance, offers around 300 types of beer. For something different, ask to try

USEFUL DINING PHRASES

I'd like a table for (two), please
Graag een tafel voor (twee) personen, alstublieft
Khraakh ayn taa-fel for (tway) persoanen, als-too-bleeft

Could I have the bill, please?
De rekening, alstublieft?
De ray-ken-ing, als-too-bleeft?

Waiter!
Ober!
Oaber!

Does it have meat in it?
Zitten er vlees in?
Zitten air vlees in?

Where are the toilets?
Waar is het toilet?
Vaar is het twa-let?

○ *Bruges boasts a wide range of locally brewed beers*

a refreshing white *witbier*, a Trappist beer such as Chimay, the tangy lambic, fizzier and sharper Geuze or Kriek, which is lambic beer flavoured with cherries. Beware, however, of getting carried away with the sampling. Some Belgian beers are very strong; any beer labelled *tripel* can be 8–12 per cent in strength.

Entertainment & nightlife

Bruges is a small city and quiet as a rule, but it still has enough to keep all but the wildest party animal happy in the evening. Although many restaurants stop serving food around 22.00, there are plenty of places you can get a snack and a drink late into the night – some bars only close when the last person has left. Nightclubs wouldn't rival those of larger cities, but there are some

⬤ The wonderful old Cinema Liberty on Kuipersstraat

"]

excellent bars playing live or recorded music including jazz, blues and contemporary sounds.

The liveliest times to visit the city are during festivals, particularly the Cactus Festival, Klinkers and the Brugges Festival of World Music (see page 10). If you miss them, don't despair. The **Muziekcentrum Cactus** (Cactus Music Centre ⓐ Sint-Sebastiaanstraat 4 ❶ 050 33 20 14 ⓦ www.cactusmusic.be) puts on a diverse range of contemporary music throughout the year and several cafés and restaurants around town also offer live music.

Concerts of classical music usually take place in the Concertgebouw at 't Zand (see page 77), a huge auditorium with state-of-the-art facilities built in 2002. A more intimate, atmospheric venue for classical music is the converted church of **Joseph Ryelandtzaal** (ⓐ Achiel van Ackerplein, off Ezelstraat ❶ 050 44 86 86). Other churches regularly host concerts so look out for posters or in listings magazines. The city's local symphony orchestra is the Symfonieorkest Vlaanderen.

If you're into dance, try to coincide your visit with December's dance festival (see pages 11 & 12), which delivers exciting programmes of classical and contemporary performances from internationally renowned dancers and musicians. Dance is also regularly on the bill at the **Stadsschouwburg** (City Theatre ⓐ Vlamingstraat 29 ❶ 050 44 30 60 ⓦ www.cultuurcentrumbrugge.be). For jazz, head for **De Werf Arts Centre** (ⓐ Werfstraat 108 ❶ 050 33 05 29 ⓦ www.dewerf.be).

Cinema is popular in Bruges, with films generally being shown in their original language with subtitles. The **Lumière** cinema near Markt (ⓐ Sint-Jacobsstraat 36 ❶ 050 34 34 65 ⓦ www.lumiere.be) shows art-house films on three large screens, with great sound and comfort. The **Kinepolis**, just outside the city centre, shows the latest releases (ⓐ Koning Albert I-laan 200 ❶ 050 30 50 00 ⓦ www. kinepolis.be ⓝ Bus: 27).

Sport & relaxation

SPECTATOR SPORTS
Football
Club Brugge is based at the 29,000 capacity Jan Breydel stadium.
Tickets cost between €20 and €50. Cercle Brugge is a smaller local team.
ⓐ Olympialaan 74 ⓣ 050 40 21 35 ⓦ www.clubbrugge.be ⓝ Bus: 5, 15
to Sint-Andries Kerk; special bus from railway station on match days

PARTICIPATION SPORTS
Cycling
You can hire bicycles at **Bruges Railway Station** (ⓐ Left luggage desk
ⓣ 050 30 23 29) or at one of several bike shops around town. Try **De
Ketting** (ⓐ Gentpoortstraat 23 ⓣ 050 34 41 96), **Bauhaus Bike Rental**
(ⓐ Langestraat 135 ⓣ 050 34 10 93) or **Eric Popelier** (ⓐ Mariastraat 26
ⓣ 050 34 32 62). Remember to take your passport and enough money
for a deposit. Some hotels offer free bicycle hire.
  Quasimundo (ⓣ 050 33 07 75 ⓦ www.quasimundo.com) offers fun
bike tours of Bruges or the surrounding area. Tours run daily (Mar–
Oct) and there are also evening tours. Booking recommended.

Golf
Damme Golf & Country Club is just outside Damme. ⓐ Doornstraat
16 ⓣ 050 35 35 72 ⓦ www.dammegolf.be ⓛ 08.30–18.00 daily
(summer); 09.00–17.00 daily (winter)

Swimming
There are three public swimming pools, all outside of the city
centre: **Jan Guilini** (ⓐ Keizer Karelstraat 43 ⓣ 050 31 35 54 ⓝ Bus: 9 to
Graafvisartpark), **Interbad** (ⓐ Veltemweg 35 ⓣ 050 35 07 77 ⓝ Bus:

10 to Sint-Andreaslyceum) or **Olympiabad** (ⓐ Doornstraat 110
ⓘ 050 39 02 00 ⓛ Hours vary ⓝ Bus: 25 to Jan Breydel).

Walking

Bruges is compact and walking around the city is a pleasant way
to exercise as well as to get about. To get your heart pumping
a little harder walk to the village of Damme (see page 104) or climb
the 366 steps to the top of Belfort (see page 63).

RELAXATION

Sauna

Sauna Mozaiek Sauna, whirlpool, infrared cabin, Turkish steam bath
and a relaxation room. Hors d'oeuvres and drinks are included in
the price and you can purchase beauty products in the shop.
ⓐ Dorpstraat 6 ⓘ 050 67 58 07 ⓦ www.badhuismozaiek.be
ⓛ 09.00–23.00 daily

⬥ *Bruges is a compact city that's easy to cycle around*

Accommodation

Bruges boasts an excellent range of accommodation to suit all tastes and budgets. Many hotels, even the cheaper ones, are on canals or housed in lovely old buildings. There are plenty of upmarket hotels around if you want to splash out on a romantic weekend, and many affordable B&Bs and hostels. In high season, however, you should still book well in advance.

As a general rule, the nearer a hotel is to Markt, the more expensive it will be. It's still worth staying within easy walking distance of the city centre, however, to limit travel time. You can often find good deals by contacting tour operators or Eurostar, particularly in low season and during the week rather than at weekends.

Some of the city's hotels include a buffet breakfast in their rates, but others charge a hefty supplement, so it's wise to check before making a booking.

The Bruges tourist information website (🔵 www.brugge.be) carries a comprehensive list of hotels and self-catering apartments and their facilities. It also provides links to the hotels' own websites. For B&B listings, see 🔵 www.brugge-bedandbreakfast.com

Most hotels are close enough to the station to walk or, if carrying heavy bags, you could take a taxi.

PRICE CATEGORIES
Based on the average price of a double room per night, including breakfast:
£ up to €140 ££ €140–200 £££ over €200

HOTELS

Adornes £ On St Anna Canal in a group of 16th- and 18th-century houses, a short walk from Markt. Free bicycles for guests. ⓐ Sint-Annarei 26 (Northeast of Markt) ⓣ 050 34 13 36 ⓦ www.adornes.be ⓝ Bus: 4, 14 to Gouden Handstraat

Botaniek £ A small, quiet hotel in an 18th-century house between Astrid Park and the Dijver. ⓐ Waalsestraat 23 (South of Markt) ⓣ 050 34 14 24 ⓦ www.botaniek.be ⓝ Bus: 6, 16 to Vismarkt

Ter Brughe £ In a 16th-century house on a canal north of Markt. Go for one of the more expensive rooms. ⓐ Oost-Gistelhof 2 (Northeast of Markt) ⓣ 050 34 03 24 ⓦ www.hotelterbrughe.com ⓝ Bus: 4, 14 to Gouden Handstraat; bus: 1, 13 to Kipstraat

Malleberg £–££ A charming family hotel, on a street off Burg, to the east. Free Internet access. ⓐ Hoogstraat 7 (Markt & Burg)

⬤ *A hotel sign for more affordable accommodation*

🕿 050 34 41 11 🌐 www.malleberg.be Ⓝ Bus: 1, 2, 5, 6, 9, 11, 15, 16 to
Wollestraat; bus: 1, 2, 3, 4, 11, 12, 13, 14 to Markt

Martin's Brugge ££ A modern hotel near Markt, trendily decorated,
with a good bar and comfortable rooms. Ⓐ Oude Burg 5 (Markt &
Burg) 🕿 050 44 51 11 🌐 www.martins-hotels.com Ⓝ Bus: 1, 2, 5, 6, 9,
11, 15, 16 to Wollestraat; bus: 1, 2, 3, 4, 11, 12, 13, 14 to Markt

Martin's Relais (Oud Huis Amsterdam) ££ Recently taken over by
the Belgian Martin's group, this atmospheric hotel, in 18th-century
buildings, boasts large, comfortable rooms (some with canal views,
others with a garden view, the odd one with a balcony) in a quiet
area just north of Markt. Ⓐ Genthof 4a 🕿 050 34 18 10 🌐 www.
martins-hotels.com Ⓝ Bus: 4, 14 to Jan Van Eyckplein

Oud Huis De Peellaert ££–£££ In an imposing old mansion, this is a
good base for sightseeing and has spacious rooms. Ⓐ Hoogstraat 20
(Markt & Burg) 🕿 050 33 78 89 🌐 www.depeellaert.com Ⓝ Bus: 6, 16
to Vismarkt; bus: 1, 2, 3, 4, 11, 12, 13, 14 to Markt

Pandhotel ££–£££ Well-located, exceptionally stylish boutique hotel,
family-run, with beautifully decorated rooms and a cosy lounge and bar.
Ⓐ Pandreitje 16 (South of Markt) 🕿 050 34 06 66 🌐 www.pandhotel.com
Ⓝ Bus: 6, 16 to Vismarkt; bus: 1, 2, 3, 4, 11, 12, 13, 14 to Markt

Die Swaene ££–£££ One of Bruges's most romantic hotels, situated
on a pretty canal. Rooms are individually designed, and the hotel
also has an excellent restaurant (Pergola Kaffee) on the other side
of the canal. Ⓐ Stenhouwersdijk (Markt & Burg) 🕿 050 34 27 98
🌐 www.dieswaene.com; www.slh.com Ⓝ Bus: 6, 16 to Vismarkt

● *Rich furnishings are in abundance at the elegant Pandhotel*

Kempinski Hotel Dukes' Palace £££ The smartest address in town, with everything – including spa, pool, garden and fine dining restaurant – you would associate with a luxury hotel in a restored palace. It's well situated but also very peaceful. ❸ Prinsenhof 8 (Markt & Burg) ❶ 050 44 78 88 ⓦ www.kempinski-bruges.com ⓝ Bus: 3, 4, 6, 10, 13, 14, 16 to 't Zand or Sint-Salvatorskerk

Relais Ravenstein £££ Opened in 2004, this modern hotel boasts contemporary décor, large rooms, state-of-the-art facilities, a very good restaurant and a welcoming bar with a canal terrace. ❸ Molenmeers 11

(Northeast of Markt) 📞 050 47 69 47 🌐 www.relaisravenstein.be
🚌 Bus: 6, 16 to Coupure

De Tuilerieën £££ One of Bruges's most prestigious traditional hotels.
Service is friendly and some rooms overlook the Dijver Canal. It is close
to the city centre and has a small swimming pool. 📍 Dijver 7 (South
of Markt) 📞 050 34 36 91 🌐 www.hoteltuilerieen.com 🚌 Bus: 1, 11 to
Eekhoutpoort; bus: 1, 2, 3, 4, 11, 12, 13, 14 to Markt

BED & BREAKFAST

AM/PM £ For a comfortable but inexpensive stay, try this stylishly
renovated 1905 town house, designed by the architect owner.
📍 Singel 10 (South of Markt) 📞 0485 07 10 03 🌐 www.bruges-
bedandbreakfast.com 🚌 Short walk from station

🔺 AM/PM B&B is a cheap and comfortable option over some hotels

Huyze Hertsberge ££ Centrally located next to a canal, with a pleasant garden. ❸ Hertsbergestraat 8 (Markt & Burg) ❶ 0475 45 77 07 Ⓦ www.huyzehertsberge.be Ⓝ Bus: 6, 16 to Vismarkt; bus: 1, 2, 3, 4, 11, 12, 13, 14 to Markt

HOSTELS & CAMPSITES

Bauhaus International Youth Hostel £ Fairly close to Markt, with its own restaurant. ❸ Langestraat 135–137 (Northeast of Markt) ❶ 050 34 10 93 Ⓦ www.bauhaus.be Ⓝ Bus: 6, 16 to Kruispoort

Camping Memling £ The only campsite in Bruges, beyond the outer canal east of the city centre. ❸ Veltemweg 109 (Northeast of Markt) ❶ 050 35 58 45 Ⓦ www.campingmemling.be Ⓝ Bus: 58 to Sint-Kruis-Vossensteert; bus: 10 to Sint-Kruis Watertoren

Charlie Rockets £ Central and lively with a bar and pool tables. ❸ Hoogstraat 19 (Markt & Burg) ❶ 050 33 06 60 Ⓦ www.charlie rockets.com Ⓝ Bus: 6, 16 to Vismarkt; bus: 1, 2, 3, 4, 11, 12, 13, 14 to Markt

Passage £ One of the best hostels, close to St Saviour's Cathedral and all the other main attractions. Good bar. ❸ Dweersstraat 26 (South of Markt) ❶ 050 34 02 32 Ⓦ www.passagebruges.com Ⓝ Bus: 1, 2, 3, 4, 5, 6, 9, 11, 12, 13, 14, 15, 16 to Sint-Salvatorskerk or 't Zand

Snuffel Backpacker Hostel £ Relaxed hostel northwest of Markt, with a bar and bikes for rent. ❸ Ezelstraat 47–49 (Northeast of Markt) ❶ 050 33 31 33 Ⓦ www.snuffel.be Ⓝ Bus: 3, 13 to Ezelpoort

THE BEST OF BRUGES

Since central Bruges is so compact, you can easily enjoy most of the main sights in a long weekend. Just wandering around can be as rewarding as visiting museums and churches, or you can take walking, cycling, horse-drawn carriage and canal tours around town.

TOP 10 ATTRACTIONS

- **Markt & Belfort** The market square and bell tower are the hub of old Bruges (see pages 60 & 63).

- **Groeninge Museum** Bruges's main museum, with a splendid collection of Flemish art from the Renaissance to the present day (see page 82).

- **Sint-Janshospitaal (St John's Hospital) & Memling in Sint-Jan Hospitaalmuseum** The medieval hospital complex not only is attractive in itself but also houses an excellent gallery with paintings by Hans Memling, and a fascinating old pharmacy (see pages 78 & 83).

- **Burg** This square houses the Heiligbloed Basiliek (Basilica of the Holy Blood), the 12th-century church where the supposed relic of the blood of Christ is kept. Opposite the basilica is the grand Stadhuis (Town Hall) (see pages 60, 64 & 66).

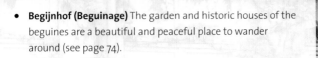

- **Begijnhof (Beguinage)** The garden and historic houses of the beguines are a beautiful and peaceful place to wander around (see page 74).

- **Gruuthuse Museum** The huge mansion of the Lords of Gruuthuse dates from when Bruges was at its commercial zenith (see page 82).

- **Onze-Lieve-Vrouwekerk (Church of Our Lady)** This vast medieval church, with its 122-m (400-ft)-high spire, is one of the city's main landmarks, and contains a sculpture by Michelangelo (see page 78).

- **Canal walk** Taking a walk or picnicking around any of Bruges's canals will open up a world of unexpected vistas.

- **Canal boat trip** Get a different perspective on Bruges with a short trip on the canals (see page 58), or take a boat to the nearby village of Damme (see page 106).

- **Horse-drawn carriage ride** Touristy in the extreme, but nevertheless a great way to see Bruges's main attractions (see page 58).

🔽 *Old windows in Bruges*

Suggested itineraries

HALF-DAY: BRUGES IN A HURRY

Half a day isn't really enough to do justice to the city, but it will tempt you to come back. Walk around Markt and Burg (see page 60), then visit the Groeninge Museum (see page 82), the Gruuthuse Museum (see page 82) and the Onze-Lieve-Vrouwekerk (Church of Our Lady, see page 78). If you would rather stay outside, take a canal trip (see page 58) or a horse-drawn carriage ride (see page 58). Leave time for mussels and chips in a pretty square, washed down by local Belgian beer.

ONE DAY: TIME TO SEE A LITTLE MORE

You'll have just enough time to fit in the peaceful hospital complex of Sint-Janshospitaal and the adjacent Archaeology Museum (see pages 78 & 81), or you could pop into the Memling in Sint-Jan Hospitaalmuseum (see page 83), Begijnhof (see page 74) or De Halve Maan Brewery (see page 78). Stroll along the canals, find a cosy restaurant and try some local specialities such as *waterzooi* or raw herring. Pick up gifts or designer accessories along Steenstraat and stop off at a bar on Markt for a celebratory glass of gin.

2–3 DAYS: TIME TO SEE MUCH MORE

Now you can go and admire the Heiligbloed Basiliek (Basilica of the Holy Blood, see page 64), the Stadhuis (Town Hall, see page 66), and St Saviour's Cathedral (see page 44) with its treasury and collection of paintings. The nearby Concertgebouw (see page 77) often runs special exhibitions and you can get great views from the roof. Enjoy a picnic in the pretty Minnewaterpark (see page 44), then walk it off by climbing to the top of Belfort (see page 63) and be rewarded by even better views. Then tempt yourself with a visit to Choco-Story (see page 90),

the enticing chocolate museum. To get away from the crowds stroll through the peaceful St Anna district (see pages 90 & 94).

LONGER: ENJOYING BRUGES TO THE FULL

You'll have time to seek out some of Bruges's more quirky shops, such as The Bottle Shop (see page 68). If you're still hungry for museums, try the Arentshuis (Brangwyn Museum, see page 81) or the Diamant Museum (Diamond Museum, see page 77). It's also fun to visit the windmills (see page 97) and admire the city gates on Bruges's outer canal. Children of all ages will love the **Boudewijn Seapark** (ⓐ Alfons de Baeckestraat 12 ❶ 050 38 38 38 ⓦ www.boudewijnsea park.be ❶ 10.00–18.00 daily (Easter, July & Aug); 10.00–17.00 Sat & Sun (Apr & Sept); 10.00–17.00 Thur–Tues (May & June)), or you could pop to the lovely nearby village of Damme (see page 104), the historic city of Ghent (see page 114) or, for a powerful experience, the World War I battlefields at Ypres (see page 128).

● The Gruuthuse Museum bears witness to Bruges's wealthy past

Something for nothing

Bruges is small and beautiful – almost a museum in itself. It is packed with lovely old houses and public buildings, carefully restored and always free to admire from the outside. Many churches still allow free entry, so don't miss out on seeing the Basilica of the Holy Blood (see page 64), St Walburga's Church (see page 98) and **St Saviour's Cathedral** (❸ St-Salvatorkoorstraat 8 ❶ 050 33 68 41 ● 14.00–17.00 Sun–Fri). The Begijnhof (see page 74) is free to enter although there is a charge for the museum. It's also worth walking around Sint-Janshospitaal enclaves (see page 78) or the grounds of the Arentshuis Museum (see page 81) even if you don't want to pay to go inside.

People-watching is a favoured pastime in Bruges and there are numerous charming squares and atmospheric cafés in which to do it. The **Jan van Eyckplein** is one of the best places to sit and contemplate the world. You could also head for one of the city's attractive free parks. Just south of Markt, the **Astridpark** has a small pond and a colourful bandstand, and the romantic **Minnewaterpark** is built around the so-called 'Lake of Love'. If you visit Bruges during one of its many festivals, the streets provide lively, free entertainment all day long.

Restaurant prices are high around Markt, 't Zand Square, the Dijver and the Begijnhof. Food and drink are often much better and cheaper in the numerous small restaurants and cafés away from this area. Picnicking on snacks from the wonderful delicatessens and fresh produce from the food markets at Markt or 't Zand (see page 25) is a great way to get an economical meal.

If your budget doesn't match your desires in terms of shopping, stick to the window displays of Bruges's luxury designer shops, but you can pick up some great souvenirs in the markets around Markt or 't Zand.

⬥ *The Baroque interior of Sint-Walburgakerk*

When it rains

Come prepared for rain in Bruges at any time of year and don't let it spoil your visit. With an umbrella and a raincoat there is very little you can't do – even canal boats and horse-drawn carriages simply put their covers up and carry on.

A rainy day is a good reason to spend longer in Bruges's excellent museums, particularly the Groeninge Museum (see page 82), where the huge collection of Flemish art could keep you occupied for hours. A tour around the De Halve Maan Brewery (see page 78) or the Choco-Story chocolate museum (see page 90) will provide some light relief, as will the **Lamp Museum** (ⓐ Wijnzakstraat 2 ① 050 61 22 37 ⓦ www.luminadomestica.be ① 10.00–17.00 daily) just next door with the largest collection of lamps in the world. An afternoon spent in the unique Kantcentrum (Lace Centre, see page 95), in the Jerusalem Church (see page 93) or in the more exotic Diamond Museum (see page 77) will easily make you forget the weather outside.

Dull weather is also a great excuse to linger over a long lunch and appreciate the rich gastronomy that Bruges has to offer – seek out a small, typical restaurant away from the touristy centre and try the local specialities.

Wet evenings can actually be a romantic time to take a stroll along the canals with a large umbrella. If that's too brave, try to get tickets for a concert at the grand Concertgebouw (see page 77) for an unforgettable experience. Cinemas (see page 31) are another good option on a rainy night, particularly if you have children in tow. If you don't, simply find a bar and spend the evening sampling a few of the 600 types of Belgian beer on offer – 't Brugs Beertje (see page 88) has a selection of around 300 of them, as well as the local speciality flavoured gin.

▲ *Rain is the perfect excuse for a brewery tour at De Halve Maan*

On arrival

TIME DIFFERENCE

Belgium is on Central European Time, 1 hour ahead of GMT. Daylight saving applies. Clocks go forward 1 hour in late March and are turned back 1 hour in late October.

ARRIVING

By air

The nearest international airport to Bruges is **Brussels Airport** (ⓦ www.brusselsairport.be), 14 km (9 miles) outside Brussels. It has all the usual facilities including an information desk, ATMs and car hire. At the time of writing there were no direct public transport connections from Brussels Airport to Bruges.

There are four trains every hour from the station on level 1 direct to central Brussels between 05.30 & 00.30. There are regular connections to Bruges from all three stations in Brussels (Midi/Zuid, Centraal/Centrale and Nord). The total journey time from the airport to central Bruges is around 1 hour 30 minutes. See ⓦ www.b-rail.be

The regular no. 471 bus, run by **De Lijn** (ⓦ www.delijn.be), leaves roughly every 30 minutes from the airport terminal at level 0 from 05.00 to 22.00 Mon–Fri. It takes around 45 minutes to reach Brussels Nord, where you can change for a train to Bruges.

The express airport bus nos 11 & 12 run every 12–20 minutes from 05.45 to 23.00 daily, directly from the airport to Brussels city centre with a journey time of 30 minutes. Change at Schuman metro for the railway stations. This is a good option if you want to spend some time in Brussels before transferring to Bruges.

Driving to Bruges from Brussels Airport takes around 1 hour 15 minutes, depending on traffic. There are several car-hire offices at

the airport (see page 58). A taxi to Bruges can cost up to €140 one way. See Ⓦ www.taxi2airport.be

Ryanair flights land at **Charleroi Airport** (Ⓦ www.charleroi-airport.com), about an hour's drive from Brussels. There is a shuttle bus direct to Brussels Midi/Zuid station, where you can catch a train for Bruges. Beware rogue taxi drivers who may tell you the service isn't working in order to persuade you to use them instead. A taxi to Brussels can cost up to €100. **Ryanair** (Ⓦ www.ryanair.com) can also arrange private transfers to Brussels from €15 per person.

By rail

Eurostar trains terminate at Brussels Midi/Zuid station. You can change there for a train to Bruges, which leaves roughly every half

🔺 *Bruges has regular rail connections to Brussels*

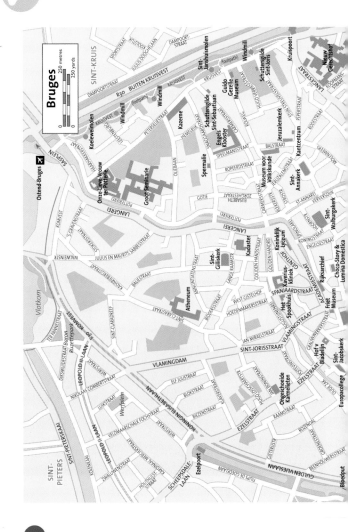

Bruges

0 — 250 metres
0 — 250 yards

SINT-KRUIS

Ostend-Bruges

Vlotkom

SINT-PIETERS

Koeleweimolen
Windmill
Windmill
Windmill
Sint-Janshuismolen
Windmill
Schuttersgilde Sint-Joris
Kruispoort
Nieuw Gerechtshof
LANGESTRAAT

Kazerne
Schuttersgilde Sint-Sebastiaan
Guido Gezelle Museum
Engels Klooster
Jeruzalemkerk
Kantcentrum
Spermalie
Museum voor Volkskunde
Sint-Annakerk
Onze-Lieve-Vrouw ter Potterie
Groot Seminarie
Sint-Walburgakerk
LANGEREI
LANGEREI
Sint-Gilliskerk
Atheneum
Kadaster
Koninklijk Lyceum
Sint-Xaveriuskliniek
Rijksarchief
Choco-Story & Lumina Domestica
Het Spookhuis
Friet Museum
Hof v Bladelijn
Sint-Jacobskerk
VLAMINGDAM
Ongeschoeide Karmelieten
Europacollege
SINT-JORISSTRAAT
KONINGIN ELISABETHLAAN
LEOPOLD II-LAAN
EZELSTRAAT
Westplein
Ezelpoort
SCHEPSDALE LAAN
GULDEN VLIESLAAN
Bloedput

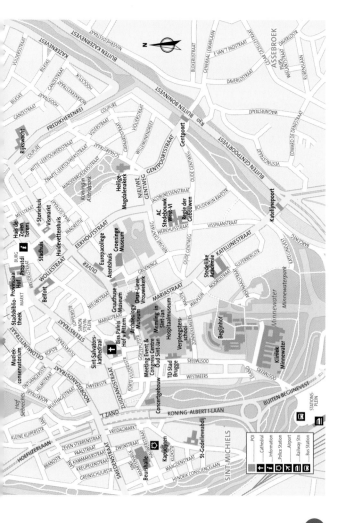

an hour and takes around 55 minutes. If you select 'Any Belgian Station' when booking on the Eurostar website (ⓦ www.eurostar.com), you can travel to and from Bruges at a reduced cost on your days of arrival and departure using your Eurostar ticket. General train information: ❶ 02 528 28 28 ⓦ www.b-rail.be

Bruges Railway Station (ⓐ Stationsplein ❶ 050 30 23 29 ⓛ 05.00–22.50 daily) is a 20-minute walk or a 10–15-minute bus journey from the centre. The station has a tourist information point, café, supermarket and taxi rank. Several bus lines (see map, page 54) leave regularly for Markt and other central areas between about 06.00 & 20.00. ❶ Beware of pickpockets around the station

🔺 Bruges's city centre is best left to horse-drawn carriages and pedestrians

By road

The main bus and coach terminal in Bruges is next to the railway
station on Stationsplein.

Bringing a car into central Bruges is not recommended. The city
centre is small and not car-friendly, with tricky one-way systems
and limited parking. Large car parks are located at 't Zand, Biekorf,
Begijnhof, Pandreitje and at the railway station, but they fill up fast,
particularly in summer and at the weekend. The railway station car
park is the best and cheapest option.

Street parking in the centre is metered from 09.00 to 19.00
with a time limit of two hours. In 'blue zones' you can park for up
to four hours with a blue parking disc, available from garages and
tobacconists, or free of charge on Sundays and Belgian public
holidays (if you can find a space!). Be careful not to incur a hefty
fine by parking in resident-only bays.

FINDING YOUR FEET

Bruges is a relaxed and friendly place and you will soon feel at
home strolling around the narrow medieval streets. Cars are
restricted in the centre and travel slowly so roads are generally safe,
but do be aware that bicycles are allowed to go in the opposite
direction down a one-way street.

Many locals speak English and will happily give directions if
you get lost. As with any city, however, be aware of pickpockets in
crowded areas; keep handbags and wallets hidden and valuables
locked in a hotel safe.

ORIENTATION

The oval-shaped centre of Bruges is only 3 km (less than 2 miles)
across, surrounded by the outermost canal. The heart of the city is

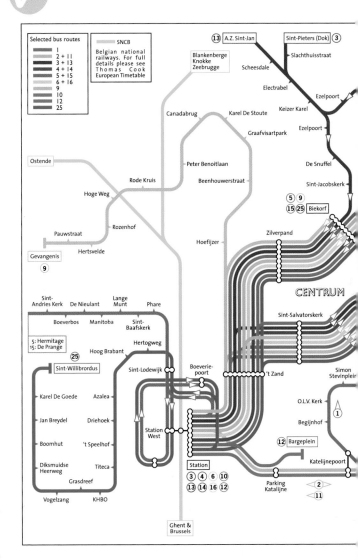

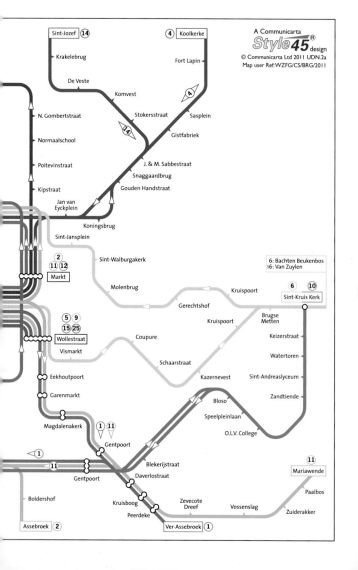

Markt. Keep the Belfort – the belfry of the market hall in Markt – as your main landmark; you can see it from most areas in the city. For another point of reference, scan the sky for the spires of the Church of Our Lady and St Saviour's Cathedral and for the huge terracotta-coloured Concertgebouw at 't Zand.

GETTING AROUND

It takes no longer than 45 minutes, at a leisurely pace, to walk from one end of Bruges to the other. Traffic is slow in the old, one-way streets so walking and cycling (see page 32) are definitely your best transport options. Note that cyclists can go in the opposite direction down one-way streets but are not allowed in pedestrianised areas.

There are several buses in the centre but these are generally only useful for getting to the railway station. Single tickets cost €1.60

IF YOU GET LOST, TRY...

Do you speak English?
Spreekt u Engels?
Spraykt-oo Eng-els?

Is this the way to...?
Is dit de weg naar...?
Is dit de vekh naar...?

Could you point it out on the map?
Kunt u het op de kaart aanwijzen?
Kunt oo het op de kaart aan-wayezen?

⬥ *A canal trip is a great way to see the city*

from the driver or €1.20 if bought in advance. More economical multi-ride tickets can be obtained from the De Lijn office at the railway station (🕐 10.30–17.45 Mon–Fri, 10.00–17.15 Sat) or from a ticket machine. Tickets must be validated in the machine when you board the bus. The Brugge City Card (see page 20) also allows you to travel at a discount.

The only two taxi ranks are at Markt and the railway station. You can't hail taxis. They tend to be expensive and drivers expect a 10–15 per cent tip. To book a taxi, call **Rony's Taxis** (📞 050 33 38 81) or **Taxis Brugge** (📞 050 33 44 44).

An excellent way to see the city centre from the water is to take a 30-minute canal tour. Regular tours leave 10.00–18.00 March–November and cost around €6.90 per adult. There are five landing stages, including one at the back of Belfort, one by the Town Hall and one near the Church of Our Lady.

Horse-drawn carriages are also popular, with trips from Markt (opposite the Belfort) to Begijnhof lasting 30 minutes and costing around €35 for a four- or five-person carriage.

City Tour Brugge (🕿 050 35 50 24 🌐 www.citytour.be) offers guided 50-minute minibus tours around Bruges with commentary in the language of your choice. Regular tours leave Markt on the hour from 10.00 until 16.00 (Jan & Feb), 17.00 (Mar, Nov & Dec), 19.00 (Apr–June), 20.00 (July–Sept), 18.00 (Oct).

You can also go on guided scooter tours from 't Santpoortje and 't Zand. The itinerary of the orange Vespas includes Damme, Knokke and other locations around the outskirts of Bruges. 🕿 0497 64 86 48 🌐 www.vespatours-brugge.be

Various tours by **Segway** are also available. 🌐 www.segway brugge.be

Car hire

Avis 🅰 Koningin Astridlaan 97 🕿 050 39 44 00 🌐 www.avis.com
Europcar 🅰 Sint-Pieterskaai 48 🕿 050 31 45 44 🌐 www.europcar.com
Hertz 🅰 Pathoekeweg 25 🕿 050 37 72 34 🌐 www.hertz.com
Luxauto 🅰 Sint-Pieterskaai 59 🕿 050 31 48 48 🌐 www.luxauto.be
Brussels Airport, as well as outlets for Hertz, Avis and Europcar, has **Sixt** (🕿 02 753 25 60 🌐 www.sixt.be).

● *The Smedenpoort (one of the city gates) in Bruges*

THE CITY OF
Bruges

Markt & Burg

Markt is both the main market square and the heart and soul of Bruges. Belfort, the towering belfry of the old market hall, is the city's most important landmark and is visible for miles around. The square is the starting point for horse-drawn carriage rides and minibus tours and there is a colourful food market on Wednesday mornings. The best place for a spot of people-watching and a classic beer or cup of coffee is the carefully restored ancient-looking **Craenenburg café** (❸ Markt 16 ❶ 050 33 34 02 Ⓦ www.craenenburg.be ⏱ 07.30–24.00 daily) on the west side of the square.

   Burg Square, just next to Markt, was the original heart of Bruges but is now much less busy. Just off Burg is the **Vismarkt** (⏱ 08.00–12.00 Tues–Sat), a market of fresh fish displayed on stone slabs. For a

GOLDEN SPURS

The 19th-century statue that stands in the centre of Markt commemorates Pieter de Coninck and Jan Breydel, who led a successful rebellion against French rule in the early 14th century. Clashes between professional French cavalry forces and the untrained Flemish militia, including around 5,500 men from in and around Bruges, culminated in the Battle of the Golden Spurs on 11 July 1302 near the Flemish town of Kortrijk. The Flemish victors chased the fleeing survivors over several kilometres before returning to a rich bounty of golden spurs from the fallen French knights. The date of 11 July is now celebrated by the Flemish community as a public holiday.

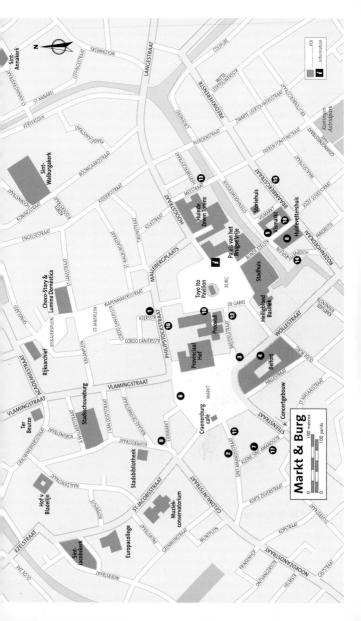

Markt & Burg

0 — 100 meters
0 — 100 yards

POI
i — Information

Map labels

Sint-Annakerk

Sint-Walburgakerk

Choco-Story & Lumina Domestica

Rijksarchief

Ter Beurze

Stadsschouwburg

Hof v Bladelijn

Stadsbibliotheek

Muziek-conservatorium

Sint-Jacobskerk

Europacollege

Huis de Zeven Torens

Palês van het Brugse Vrije

Stadhuis

St:nhuis

Vismarkt

Huidevettershuis

Toyo Ito Pavilion

BURG

Heiligbloed Basiliek

Proostdij

Provinciaal Hof

Craenenburg café

Belfort

Concertgebouw

MARKT

Streets

MOLENMEERS
LANGESTRAAT
COUPURE
ST ANNAREI
EEKHOUTSTRAAT
SINT-MAARTENSPLEIN
VERVERSDIJK
GROENEI
VLAMINCKSTRAAT
WITTE LEERTOUWERSSTR
ZWARTE LEERTOUWERSSTR
PREDIKHERENSTR
HOOGSTRAAT
KONINGIN ASTRIDPARK
VELDSTRAAT
KONINGSTRAAT
GENTHOFSTRAAT
BOOMGAARDSTRAAT
RIDDERSTRAAT
TWIJNSTRAAT
KELKSTRAAT
MEESTRAAT
VLAMINGSTRAAT
PEERDENSTRAAT
FREREN FONTEINSTRAAT
WALPLEIN
JOZEF SUVÉESTRAAT
ENGELSESTRAAT
GIELIAENSTRAAT
ST-WALBURGASTRAAT
GROENERI
SINT-WEYDS-STRAAT
BRAAMBERGSTRAAT
KROM GENTHOF
ST-JANSSTRAAT
ST-JANSPLEIN
WAPENMAKERSTRAAT
ST-JANSPLEIN
VISMARKT
ROZENHOEDKAAI
HANDBOOGSTRAAT
EIERMARKT
ACADEMIESTRAAT
VLAMINGSTRAAT
PHILIPSTOCKSTRAAT
KEERSSTR
CORDO EANIERSSTR
CORDO EANIERSSTRAAT
DE GARRE
BLINDE EZELSTR
HUIDENVETTERSSTR
NAALDENSTRAAT
KUIPERSSTRAAT
GRAUWWERKERSSTRAAT
ROBIJNSTRAAT
GELDMUNTSTRAAT
BREIDELSTRAAT
WOLLESTRAAT
HALLESTRAAT
OUDE BURG
STANDAAKSTRAAT
STEENSTRAAT
EZELSTRAAT
MOERSTRAAT
LOPPEMSTRAAT
ST-JACOBSSTRAAT
PALMSTRAAT
GEERWIJNSTRAAT
MUNTPLEIN
SINT-AMANDSTRAAT
KLEINE SINT-AMANDSTR
KORTE ZILVERSTRAAT
KORPERSTRAAT
ZILVERSTRAAT
JOHNSTRAAT
NOORDZANDSTRAAT
KOPSTRAAT
HEMSTR
GISTSTR
ONTVANGERSSTRAAT
OUDE ZAK

pretty canal-side walk you can't beat Groenerei, just round the corner from Burg.

Information about many of the sights and cultural attractions in the area can be found on Ⓦ www.brugge.be

⬥ *The Belfort towers above the city*

SIGHTS & ATTRACTIONS

Belfort (Belfry)

The spectacular 83-m (272-ft)-high tower, the belfry of the city's market hall, came to symbolise Bruges's importance when it was at its wealthiest. The lower sections of the building date back to the 13th century and the bell tower was added 200 years later.

If you can manage the 366 spiral steps up and down it's well worth making the effort; the views from the enclosed area at the

PROCESSION OF THE HOLY BLOOD

The Heiligbloedprocessie (Procession of the Holy Blood) takes place in Bruges every year on Ascension Day, attracting tens of thousands of visitors from around the world. The relic of the Holy Blood, normally housed in the Heiligbloed Basiliek, is taken on a mile-long procession through the city in the same grand style as it has been since the beginning of the 14th century.

One of the great religious pageants of Europe, the procession is a highly ceremonial and important event in the Bruges calendar. Huge floats move slowly through the streets, with costumed participants enacting scenes from the Bible. Over 1,500 local citizens take part, dressed either in biblical clothes or in medieval costumes.

The parade leaves at 15.00 and takes around 2 hours 30 minutes, starting and ending at the Concertgebouw. Tickets for seats (either in covered stands or on benches) can be obtained from the tourist office.

top are superb. On the way up, you will also get to see the treasury, the clock mechanism, and finally an intricate piece of machinery that controls the carillon of 47 bells that chimes every 15 minutes. Get there early to avoid the queues. ⓐ Markt 7 🕐 09.30–17.00 daily (last admission 16.15) ⓘ Admission charge

Heiligbloed Basiliek (Basilica of the Holy Blood)

Tucked away in a corner of Burg Square is this tiny church with an ornately decorated façade and two chapels. On the ground floor lies St Basil's Chapel, completed in 1149 in austere medieval Romanesque style. In sharp contrast is the neo-Gothic chapel upstairs, rebuilt in the 19th century and housing the precious relic of the Holy Blood along with other religious objects and paintings in a small treasury. ⓐ Burg 15 🕐 09.30–11.50, 14.00–17.50 daily (summer); 10.00–11.50, 14.00–15.50 Thur–Tues, 10.00–11.50 Wed (winter) ⓘ Admission charge for treasury

Provinciaal Hof (Provincial Palace House)

Dominating the east side of Markt is the neo-Gothic Provinciaal Hof, the regional government building for West Flanders, of which Bruges is the capital. It was built in the late 19th century after a neoclassical building on the same site was destroyed by fire. You can see a painting of the earlier building in the Groeninge Museum (see page 82). Earlier still, the site was home to a late 13th-century *waterhalle*, a covered hall over a canal where goods were unloaded from barges. This was pulled down in 1789.

The building now hosts occasional temporary exhibitions, seminars and concerts. There are plans to turn it into a history museum from late 2012, with virtual displays using film, images and light effects. Visit the tourist office for details. ⓐ Markt 3

◔ *The façade of the Heiligbloed Basiliek is intricately decorated*

Toyo Ito Pavilion

In startling contrast to the carefully restored old buildings around
it is the Toyo Ito Pavilion, designed by innovative Japanese architect
Toyo Ito in 2002. The 22-m (72-ft) tunnel-shaped pavilion is made of
glass and honeycombed aluminium. There is much discussion about
how best to use it in future.

CULTURE

Paleis van het Brugse Vrije (Palace of Bruges Liberty)

Built in 1525, this palace was originally the administrative centre
for the semi-autonomous area of Bruges Liberty in the Middle Ages.
When local rule was abolished by the French during the 18th-century
Revolutionary Wars, the building became the city's courthouse.
It retained this function until the 1980s but now houses Bruges's
archives. The façade facing the square dates from the early 18th
century but the walls facing the neighbouring canal are original.

It is worth paying the small admission charge to see the Renaissance
Chamber inside, once the meeting place for the city's aldermen.
Here you will find a huge, impressive fireplace of oak, alabaster
and marble, designed in the 16th century by Lanceloot Blondel.

The charge includes an audio-guide and entry to the Stadhuis
next door (see below). ❸ Burg 11a 🕐 09.30–12.30, 13.30–17.00 Tues–
Sat ❶ Admission charge

Stadhuis (Town Hall)

Bruges's grand Town Hall dates back to 1376, making it the oldest
municipal building in all of Flanders. It has been restored on several
occasions, however, leaving only the original vaulted wooden ceiling
of the Gothic Hall, erected in 1385, untouched. The paintings on the

⬤ *At the centre of Burg is the Stadhuis*

walls of this vast council chamber depict the history of Bruges and date from the 19th century.

Next door you will find an interesting collection of artefacts, maps and other illustrations of the city's history. There are further exhibits, including paintings, on the ground floor. An audio-guide and entry to the Paleis van het Brugse Vrije (see opposite) are included in the small admission charge. ⓐ Burg 12 ⏰ 09.30–17.00 Tues–Sat ❶ Admission charge

RETAIL THERAPY

The streets around Markt – Steenstraat, Wollestraat and Geldmuntstraat – contain the best of Bruges's shops. Steenstraat is

packed with top clothes shops and chocolate shops. Wollestraat has some chic stores and several lace shops. For souvenirs head to Breidelstraat. Hoogstraat, good for antiques and designer items, is just off Burg Square.

The Bottle Shop Hundreds of different brands of beer as well as gin. Also sells souvenir T-shirts and prints. Wollestraat 13 050 34 99 80 10.00–18.30 Wed–Mon

Callebert Interior design and gift shop. Wollestraat 25 050 33 50 61 www.callebert.be 15.00–18.00 Sun & Mon, 10.00–12.00, 14.00–18.00 Tues–Sat

Chocolaterie De Burg Chocolate, biscuits and sweet treats. Burg 15 050 33 52 32 10.00–18.00 Mon–Sat, 11.00–18.00 Sun

Deldycke Excellent if pricey delicatessen. Wollestraat 23 050 33 43 35 09.00–14.00, 15.00–18.30 daily

Delvaux Eye-wateringly expensive but beautifully designed handbags. Corner of Wollestraat & Breidelstraat 050 49 01 31 www.delvaux.com 10.00–18.00 Mon–Sat

Javana A charming coffee and tea shop also selling coffee makers, teapots and mugs. Steenstraat 6 050 33 36 05 www.javana.be 10.00–18.00 Mon–Sat

Juliette's Cookies Freshly made traditional biscuits. Wollestraat 31a 050 34 84 40 www.juliettes.be 11.00–18.00 Sun & Mon, 10.00–18.00 Tues–Sat

The Lace Garden (Maison Pickery) Standing out from the many mediocre lace shops, this is one of the best places for high-quality handmade lace. ➌ Breidelstraat 8 ☏ 050 33 07 24 ⓦ www.maison pickery.com

Oil & Vinegar Delectable Mediterranean foodstuffs. ➋ Geldmuntstraat 11 ☏ 050 34 56 50 ⓦ www.oilvinegar.com ⏱ 10.00–18.00 Mon–Sat

Olivier Strelli Men's fashion by Olivier Strelli, a figurehead of Belgian fashion design creativity. Ladies' fashion is at his other outlet at Eiermarkt 3. ➌ Geldmuntstraat 19 ☏ 050 33 26 75 ⓦ www.strelli.be ⏱ 11.00–18.00 Mon, 10.00–18.00 Tues–Sat

TAKING A BREAK

One of the best places to buy the renowned Belgian chips is actually the small kiosk in front of the Belfort. If you prefer to sit down, try:

Het Dagelijks Brood £ ❶ Bakery franchise serving great breakfasts around big communal tables. Also serves lunch or tea to eat in or take away. ➋ Philipstockstraat 21 ☏ 050 33 60 50 ⓦ www.lepainquotidien.be ⏱ 08.00–18.00 Wed–Mon

Sandwicherie St-Amandje £ ❷ A bright, modern place with tables outside, serving baguettes, soups and salads. ➋ Sint-Amandsstraat 33 ☏ 050 33 06 65 ⓦ www.sintamandje.be ⏱ 09.15–19.00 Mon–Sat

The Olive Tree £–££ ❸ Greek restaurant serving traditional Mediterranean food with a contemporary twist in atmospheric

surroundings. ⓐ Wollestraat 3 ⓣ 050 33 00 81 ⓦ www.theolivetree-brugge.com ⓛ 11.30–15.00, 18.00–23.00 Mon, Wed & Thur, 11.30–15.00, 18.00–24.00 Fri–Sun

Riva del Sole £–££ ❹ The Italian chef offers some classic European dishes. ⓐ Wollestraat 22 ⓣ 050 34 33 30 ⓦ www.rivadelsole.be ⓛ 12.00–14.30, 18.00–22.30 Thur–Mon, 12.00–14.30 Tues

Den Gouden Karpel ££ ❺ Cosy seafood restaurant near the Vismarkt (fish market) with a terrace and a shop where you can buy food to take away. ⓐ Huidenvettersplein 3–4 ⓣ 050 33 34 94 ⓦ www.dengoudenkarpel.be ⓛ Restaurant: 12.00–22.00 Tues–Sun (summer); 18.30–21.30 Tues, 12.00–14.00, 18.30–21.30 Wed–Sat, 12.00–14.00 Sun (winter); shop: 08.00–12.00, 14.00–18.30 Tues–Sat

Sint Joris ££ ❻ One of the few places on Markt with reasonable prices – which is why the locals come here. Family-run with decent Belgian food, friendly service and good-value set menus. ⓐ Markt 29 ⓣ 050 33 30 62 ⓦ www.restaurant-sintjoris.be ⓛ 10.00–22.00 daily

AFTER DARK

Markt is a wonderful place to be at night, with its floodlit Belfort and romantic walks along the Groenerei and Dijver canals. There are several good restaurants and late-night bars in the area.

RESTAURANTS
Bistro De Pompe £–££ ❼ Grills, salads, stir-fries and vegetarian dishes. ⓐ Kleine Sint-Amandsstraat 2 ⓣ 050 61 66 18 ⓦ www.bistrodepompe.be ⓛ 11.30–22.00 Tues–Sun

⬤ *The reflections of the surrounding city in the water*

't Huidevettershuis £–££ ❽ Flemish cuisine in a 17th-century building overlooking the canal. ⓐ 't Huidevettersplein 10 ☏ 050 33 95 06 ⓦ www.huidevettershuis.be ⏱ 12.00–14.30, 18.00–22.00 Mon & Wed–Fri, 12.00–22.00 Sat & Sun

Malpertuus-'t Voske £–££ ❾ Robust French cuisine and local specialities at reasonable prices. ⓐ Eiermarkt 9 ☏ 050 33 30 38 ⓦ www.malpertuus-voske.be ⏱ 11.30–15.00, 18.00–22.30 Mon–Sat

Opus Latino £–££ ❿ Fashionable and popular restaurant with a terrace, tapas, pasta and salads. ⓐ Burg 15 ☏ 050 34 72 78 ⏱ 10.30–01.00 Thur–Tues

Den Amand ££ ⓫ Cosy restaurant off Markt serving a range of international dishes. ⓐ Sint-Amandsstraat 4 ⓣ 050 34 01 22 ⓦ www.denamand.be ⓛ 12.00–14.15, 18.00–21.15 Mon, Tues & Thur–Sat

Breydel-De Coninc ££ ⓬ This popular family-run restaurant specialises in mussels – they cook them in nine different ways. ⓐ Breidelstraat 24 ⓣ 050 33 97 46 ⓛ 12.00–15.00, 18.00–22.00 Thur–Tues (last orders 21.30)

Chez Olivier ££ ⓭ Upmarket French cuisine in an intimate 16th-century building overlooking the canal. ⓐ Meestraat 9 ⓣ 050 33 36 59 ⓛ 12.00–14.00, 19.00–21.00 Mon–Wed & Fri, 19.00–21.00 Sat

Duc de Bourgogne ££ ⓮ Formal but romantic, with an old-fashioned ambience and traditional food. There are also a few bedrooms. ⓐ Huidenvettersplein 12 ⓣ 050 33 20 38 ⓦ www.ducdebourgogne.be ⓛ 19.00–21.00 Tues, 12.00–14.00, 19.00–21.00 Wed–Sat

De Gastro ££ ⓯ Elegant restaurant offering a fusion of Peruvian, British and Belgian cuisine. ⓐ Braambergstraat 6 ⓣ 050 34 15 24 ⓦ www.degastro.be ⓛ 11.00–23.00 Thur–Tues

Au Petit Grand ££ ⓰ Watch your meat or fish being grilled before your eyes. ⓐ Philipstockstraat 18 ⓣ 050 34 86 71 ⓦ www.aupetitgrand.be ⓛ 18.00–24.00 Tues–Sun

De Stove ££ ⓱ Elegant family-run restaurant with a tempting menu of French and Belgian dishes. ⓐ Kleine Sint-Amandsstraat 4 ⓣ 050 33 78 35 ⓦ www.restaurantdestove.be ⓛ 12.00–13.45, 18.45–21.30 Sat–Tues, 18.45–21.30 Wed–Fri (closed 2 weeks in Jan & June)

De Visscherie ££–£££ ⑩ Among the finest fish and seafood restaurants in Bruges, appropriately situated in the fish market. The interior is smart (there are also a few outside tables), presentation pretty, and the service very professional. ⓐ Vismarkt 8 ⓣ 050 33 02 12 ⓦ www.visscherie.be ⓛ 12.00–14.00, 19.00–22.00 Wed–Mon

BARS & CLUBS

Bistro 't Zwart Huis Background jazz in this popular 15th-century building. Food served. ⓐ Kuipersstraat 23 ⓣ 050 67 62 19 ⓦ www.bistro zwarthuis.be ⓛ Restaurant: 12.00–14.00, 16.00–24.00 Wed–Fri, 16.00–24.00 Sat & Sun; bar: 12.00–02.00 Wed–Fri, 16.00–02.00 Sat & Sun

Celtic Ireland Live music most nights and a regular Monday quiz in this lively Irish pub. ⓐ Burg 8 ⓣ 050 34 45 02 ⓛ 10.30–late daily

Charlie Rockets Packed late-opening bar in a lively hostel. ⓐ Hoogstraat 19 ⓣ 050 33 06 60 ⓦ www.charlierockets.com ⓛ 08.30–late daily

De Pub Good music and a large selection of beers and cocktails keep this bar buzzing. ⓐ Geernaartstraat 2, off Eiermarkt ⓣ 050 34 71 14 ⓛ Hours vary; open until late most nights

Staminee de Garre Specialising in local beer, this place also serves snacks. ⓐ De Garre 1 ⓣ 050 34 10 29 ⓛ 12.00–24.00 Mon & Tues, 12.00–01.00 Fri, 11.00–01.00 Sat, 11.00–24.00 Sun

Vuurmolen Draws a young crowd with all-night staying power. ⓐ Kraanplein 5 ⓣ 050 33 00 79 ⓦ www.vuurmolen.be ⓛ 09.30–06.00 Mon–Fri, 10.30–08.30 Sat, 11.30–07.00 Sun

South of Markt

South of Markt is the heart of sightseeing land. A compact area, where you are likely to spend most of your time in Bruges, it is easy and pleasant to walk around. Stroll along the canals and around the grounds of the buildings, even if you don't go inside – in particular those of the Sint-Janshospitaal, the Arentshuis and the Begijnhof. Try to see a concert or visit an exhibition at the Concertgebouw, or at least admire its audacious architectural style. On Saturday mornings 't Zand Square bustles with a large food market, so buy a picnic and head for the small, green Minnewaterpark, Astridpark or Koning Albertpark to eat it.

Information about many of the sights and cultural attractions in the area can be found on Ⓦ www.brugge.be

SIGHTS & ATTRACTIONS

Begijnhof (Beguinage)
Beguines were single women who led a religious life in small communities, originally often the widows of men who had died in the Crusades. Many beguines eventually returned to life outside. This Beguinage was founded in 1245 by Margaretha, Countess of Flanders, daughter of the crusader Count Baldwin.

The delightful little whitewashed houses which stand today date from the 17th and 18th centuries. There is also a garden in the middle of the compound, which is particularly attractive in spring, and a chapel dating from 1602. One of the houses, just inside the gate to the left as you enter, is a museum all about the lives of the beguines. The last beguine died in 1928, and the houses are now occupied by elderly local ladies, usually widows. There is also a

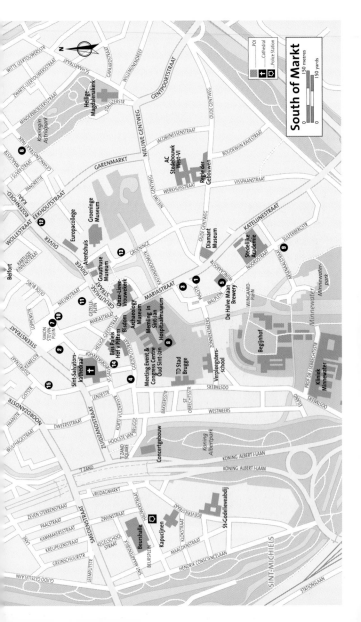

South of Markt

0   150 metres
0   150 yards

POI
Cathedral
Police Station

Locations:

Heilige-Magdalenakerk

Koningin Astridpark

AC Stedebouw West-Vl

Regie der Gebouwen

Garenmarkt

Europacollege

Groeninge Museum

Arentshuis

Gruuthuse Museum

Diamant Museum

Stedelijke Academie

Befort

Onze-Lieve-Vrouwekerk

Archeologisch Museum

Memling in Sint-Jan Hospitaalmuseum

De Halve Maan Brewery

Bisdom

Begijnhof

Meeting Event & Congress Centre Oud Sint-Jan

TD Stad Brugge

Verpleegstersschool

Kliniek Minnewater

Sint-Salvatorskathedraal

Bis Paleis Hof v Pitte

Concertgebouw

Koning Albertpark

Koning Albert I-Laan

Beurshalle

Kapucijnen

St-Godelieveabdij

Vrijdagmarkt

T Zand Square

Minnewater park

Minnewater

Sint-Michiels

community of Benedictine nuns who live here in communal accommodation.

Situated on a canal and entered via a small bridge, the Begijnhof is one of Bruges's most peaceful and sympathetic spots. It is free to walk around, though there is a small entry charge for the museum.

ⓐ Begijnhof 30 ⓑ Begijnhof: 06.30–18.30 daily; museum: 10.00–17.00 Mon–Sat, 14.30–17.00 Sun ⓘ Admission charge for museum

🔺 *The Begijnhof was once the domain of religious single women*

Concertgebouw

This state-of-the-art concert hall stands in stark contrast to
its carefully restored medieval neighbours, almost revelling in the
controversy it received when it was completed in 2002, in time for
Bruges's stint as European Capital of Culture.

An innovative structure covered with 68,000 terracotta tiles,
it stretches a massive 120 m (393 ft) from end to end and boasts
a 1,300-seat concert hall as well as a smaller chamber-music hall.
As well as important concerts and dance performances, the sixth-
floor lantern tower (Lantaarntoren) – from which you can enjoy
great views of Bruges – houses the new 'Sound Factory', opened in
late 2011 and exhibiting the sounds of the city using interactive
auditory art. Groups can book a guided tour (enquire at the office
for details) behind the scenes for an explanation of the history of
the building, the architecture and the workings of the concert hall.

The main In&Uit Brugge tourist office is situated in the building
and provides information and tickets for concerts and exhibitions
in the Concertgebouw and at other venues in the city. ⓐ 't Zand 34
ⓣ 050 47 69 99 ⓦ www.concertgebouw.be ⓛ Office: 10.00–18.00
Fri–Wed, 10.00–20.00 Thur; Lantaarntoren: 09.30–17.00 Tues–Sun

Diamant Museum (Diamond Museum)

This well-organised museum tells the fascinating history of Bruges
and its connection with diamonds. The skill of diamond polishing
allegedly originated in Bruges 500 years ago, when it was a more
important diamond centre than Amsterdam or Antwerp. Look out for
the uncut 250-carat diamond on display. There is a diamond-
polishing demonstration at 12.15 every day. ⓐ Katelijnestraat 43
ⓣ 050 34 20 56 ⓦ www.diamondmuseum.be ⓛ 10.30–17.30 daily
ⓘ Admission charge (extra for demonstration)

De Halve Maan Brewery

The 'Half-Moon' Brewery, going strong since 1856, offers 45-minute guided tours that explain how the brewing process works. A sample of their latest brand of beer, Brugse Zot, is included. The brewery also has a café where you can try a glass of Straffe Hendrick, or 'Strong Henry', or recover with a coffee and a snack. ❸ Walplein 26 ❶ 050 33 26 97 ⓦ www.halvemaan.be ❷ Tours hourly 11.00–16.00 Mon–Fri & Sun, 11.00–17.00 Sat (summer); tours at 11.00, 15.00 Mon–Fri, hourly 11.00–16.00 Sat & Sun (winter) ❶ Admission charge

Onze-Lieve-Vrouwekerk (Church of Our Lady)

The 122-m (400-ft) spire of this enormous Gothic church dominates the skyline. The church took 200 years to build, starting in 1220, and the spire was completed by 1350. As with so many buildings in Bruges, the bright interior has a mixture of architectural styles. The simple central aisle dates from the 13th century, the north aisle from the 14th century, and there are also Baroque side chapels and an ostentatious pulpit dating from 1743.

The church's main highlight, at the end of the south aisle, is Michelangelo's exquisite *Madonna and Child* sculpture (1504), donated by a local merchant in 1514. The church also has a small museum. ❸ Mariastraat ❶ 050 34 53 14 ❷ 09.30–17.00 Mon–Sat, 13.30–17.00 Sun (museum closed Mon) ❶ Free admission at north entrance for partial view of the church; admission charge at south entrance for main section of church and *Madonna and Child*

Sint-Janshospitaal (St John's Hospital)

Through the archway of the Sint-Janshospitaal site you will find a haven of calm. The complex once housed a church, convent, bakery, brewery, vegetable garden, and other facilities for the sick. Those

⬥ *The Onze-Lieve-Vrouwekerk's Gothic façade dominates the city*

who lived there devoted themselves both to healing and to God. The hospital itself functioned from 1150 to as late as 1976. Although much of the complex was demolished in 1850, the main buildings on Mariastraat date from the 13th century, when the hospital marked the edge of the city.

⬤ *The pretty courtyard at the pharmacy of Sint-Janshospitaal*

The highlight is the hospital's 17th-century pharmacy, which was originally run by nuns and kept on dispensing until 1971. Situated just to the right of the arch is an array of old drug and herb jars in a building with a pretty courtyard.

Housed in the old wards of the hospital is the Memling in Sint-Jan Hospitaalmuseum (see page 83). The adjacent Archaeology Museum is also worth a visit. You will also find several small shops and a restaurant. The grounds themselves are open 24 hours a day and are free of charge. ❸ Mariastraat 38 🕐 Pharmacy: 09.30–11.45, 14.00–17.00 Tues–Sun ❶ Admission charge for museum and pharmacy

CULTURE

Archaeology Museum

Part of the Sint-Janshospitaal complex (see page 78), this ingenious, modern museum is filled with interactive displays and is fun for both children and adults. ❸ Mariastraat 36a 🕐 09.30–12.30, 13.30–17.00 Tues–Sun ❶ Admission charge

Arentshuis (Brangwyn Museum)

The Arentshuis was originally built in 1663 but acquired its current neoclassical style in the late 18th century. Named after its last private owner Aquilin Arents de Beertegem, who died in 1980, it now belongs to the city and houses the superb Brangwyn collection of art.

Bruges-born British artist Frank Brangwyn (1867–1956) was the son of William Brangwyn, an architect and designer who helped to restore Bruges in neo-Gothic style in the 19th century. Frank Brangwyn donated many of his vivid paintings to the collection in the 1930s along with some of the furniture he had designed. Regular temporary

exhibitions on the ground floor complement the permanent collection upstairs.

The grounds, known as the **Arentspark**, are a peaceful spot in which to relax and contain one of the city's prettiest bridges along with works by the Belgian sculptor Rik Poot.

The admission charge also allows entry to the Groeninge Museum (see below). ➌ Dijver 16 🕑 09.30–17.00 Tues–Sun ❶ Admission charge

Groeninge Museum

This recently redesigned museum houses one of the finest collections of Flemish art in the world, spanning 600 years from the 15th century to the present day. The beautifully displayed works are arranged chronologically.

Highlights include Jan van Eyck's stunningly detailed *Virgin and Child with Canon Joris van der Paele* (1436), Hugo van der Goes's emotional and modern-looking *Death of the Virgin* (1481), Hans Memling's *Triptych of Willem Moreel* (1484) and the early 16th-century *The Last Judgement*, attributed to Hieronymus Bosch. Room 9 has a Magritte and other Surrealist works.

The admission charge includes an audio-guide and allows entry to the Arentshuis Museum (see page 81). ➋ Dijver 12 🕑 09.30–17.00 Tues–Sun ❶ Admission charge

Gruuthuse Museum

Visit the Gruuthuse if you want an insight into the lifestyle of wealthy inhabitants of Bruges when the city was at its most prosperous. Originally the residence of the Flemish knight Louis (Lodewijk) van Gruuthuse, the huge house was carefully restored in the late 19th and early 20th centuries. It now houses a collection of art and domestic artefacts.

FLEMISH ART COLLECTION

The Groeninge Museum is one of three historic art museums in Belgium that make up the Vlaamse Kunstcollectie, or Flemish Art Collection. The other two are the Museum of Fine Arts in Ghent and the Royal Museum of Fine Art in Antwerp. Taken together, the collections offer a unique and representative overview of fine art from the Zuidelijke Nederlanden, or Southern Low Countries, from the 15th to the 21st century. The three museums work together, sharing their expertise in order to protect these precious collections that attract international interest.

Many of the objects on display, which include furniture, paintings, tapestries and musical instruments, are stunningly well crafted. Equally impressive are the wooden ceilings, floor tiles, carvings and vast fireplaces. The enormous kitchen is another popular highlight.

The most unexpected and frightening exhibit is the guillotine on the ground floor, in full operation from 1796 right up until 1862.

The admission charge includes an audio-guide and entry to the museum in the Church of Our Lady (see page 78). Note that some parts of the museum may be closed for restoration. ⓐ Dijver 17 ⓛ 09.30–17.00 Tues–Sun ⓘ Admission charge

Memling in Sint-Jan Hospitaalmuseum

The Memling in Sint-Jan Hospitaalmuseum, housed in the old wards of the Sint-Janshospitaal (see page 78), is an imaginative conversion of the ancient space. One half of the museum focuses on the history

of the hospital through interactive terminals, historical documents, works of art, furniture and other artefacts. The other half of the museum, located in the chapel, displays six works by the Flemish master Hans Memling (1440–94), of whom the hospital was a major patron. The highlight is the triptych depicting St John the Baptist and St John the Evangelist (1479). Memling's attention to colour, composition and detail make for an interesting comparison with the other early Flemish works on display. The ticket price includes an audio-guide. ❸ Mariastraat 38 ⏱ 09.30–17.00 Tues–Sun ❶ Admission charge

RETAIL THERAPY

South of Markt is heaven for clothes shoppers, particularly in the area around St Saviour's Cathedral. There are several excellent boutiques in Steenstraat, Zuidzandstraat, Noordzandstraat and Zilverpand, as well as international chains and Belgian fashion shops. The area also contains several quality chocolate shops.

The Saturday market on 't Zand is good for cheap clothes and food, and there is a flea market along the Dijver all week during summer and at weekends in winter. For souvenir and more chocolate shops head for Katelijnestraat and Mariastraat.

De Ark van Zarren Romantic country-living shop selling attractive table linen and crockery. ❸ Zuidzandstraat 19 ☎ 050 33 77 28 ⏱ 10.00–18.30 Mon–Fri, 09.30–18.30 Sat

The Bear Necessities Teddy bears of all shapes and sizes. ❸ Groeninge 23 ☎ 050 34 10 27 🌐 www.thebearnecessities.be ⏱ 10.00–17.00 Tues–Sun

Dille en Kamille Crockery and other household goods at
competitive prices. ⓐ Simon Stevinplein 17–18 ⓣ 050 34 11 80
ⓦ www.dille-kamille.nl ⓛ 09.30–18.30 Mon–Sat, 11.00–18.30 Sun

De Kaasbolle Fantastic selection of cheeses. ⓐ Smedenstraat 11
ⓣ 050 33 71 54 ⓦ www.dekaasbolle.be ⓛ 09.00–12.30, 14.00–18.30
Mon, Tues & Thur–Sat, 09.00–12.30 Sun

Knapp Targa One of Bruges's most stylish fashion shops.
ⓐ Zuidzandstraat 22 ⓣ 050 33 31 27 ⓛ 10.00–18.30 Mon–Sat

TAKING A BREAK

The area south of Markt boasts numerous tearooms, cafés and
small restaurants, particularly around the Church of Our Lady and
the Begijnhof. If you want a cheaper meal, find a restaurant further
away from 't Zand Square.

De Bron £ ❶ One of Bruges's very few vegetarian restaurants.
ⓐ Katelijnestraat 82 ⓣ 050 33 45 26 ⓛ 11.45–14.00 Tues–Sat

Jerry's Cigar Bar £ ❷ Small, smoky modern café serving drinks
and ice creams as well as selling cigars and cigarettes. ⓐ Simon
Stevinplein 13 ⓣ 050 33 77 94 ⓦ www.jerrycigarbar.com ⓛ 08.00–
18.30 Mon–Sat, 09.00–18.30 Sun

De Proeverie £ ❸ Tearoom serving real English tea, popular
with locals and linked to the Sukerbuyc chocolate shop opposite.
ⓐ Katelijnestraat 6 ⓣ 050 33 08 87 ⓦ www.deproeverie.be
ⓛ 09.00–18.00 daily

Gauthierz £–££ ❹ In a side street near the Church of Our Lady, and very popular with locals. The set lunch is particularly good value (though choice is limited), preferably eaten on the pleasant terrace. The cuisine is Belgian/French. ⓐ Goezeputstraat 6 ❶ 050 33 13 07 ⓦ www.gauthierz.com ❶ 12.00–14.00, 18.00–22.00 Thur–Mon

De Halve Maan Brewery £–££ ❺ Snacks, drinks (including beer) and fuller meals are available at the brewery's café. ⓐ Walplein 26 ❶ 050 33 26 97 ⓦ www.halvemaan.be ❶ 10.00–18.00 daily

L'Estaminet ££ ❻ Popular place with occasional live music, just off Astridpark. ⓐ Park 5 ❶ 050 33 09 16 ❶ 11.30–late Tues, Wed & Fri–Sun, 16.00–late Thur

▲ Enjoy an outdoor café meal

Poules Moules ££ ❼ On two floors inside, with many outside tables under the trees of the square, and serving good-quality French/Belgian dishes. ⓐ Simon Stevinplein 8–9 ❶ 050 34 61 19 ⓦ www.poulesmoules.be ❶ 11.30–21.30 Tues–Sun

AFTER DARK

Most night-time dining in the area is clustered around Dijver and the Church of Our Lady. A walk along the Dijver, where many of the buildings are floodlit, can be delightful.

RESTAURANTS

B-In ££ ❽ Trendy restaurant and bar with a canal-side terrace. Serves creative, well-presented food in an ultra-modern but relaxed atmosphere. ⓐ Zonnekemeers ❶ 050 31 13 00 ⓦ www.b-in.be ❶ 12.00–14.30, 18.30–22.00 Tues–Sat

De Bekoring ££ ❾ Romantic restaurant with a fireplace and candlelit tables, offering good local cuisine. ⓐ Arsenaalstraat 55 ❶ 050 34 41 57 ❶ 12.00–14.00, 16.30–21.30 Tues–Sat, 12.00–14.00 Sun

De Koetse ££ ❿ A classic, reliable meat and fish grill restaurant. You can eat à la carte or try the menu of the month with wine included. ⓐ Oude Burg 31 ❶ 050 33 76 80 ⓦ www.dekoetse-brugge.be ❶ 12.00–14.30, 18.00–22.00 Fri–Wed

Maria van Bourgondië ££ ⓫ Authentic Burgundian and Flemish cuisine in an elegant, old-fashioned atmosphere. Outside terrace during the day. ⓐ Guido Gezelleplein 1 ❶ 050 33 20 66 ⓦ www.mariavanbourgondie.be ❶ 09.00–23.00 daily

Den Dyver ££–£££ 🕑 Excellent restaurant serving imaginative food cooked with beer. Beer is matched to the dishes and served in wine glasses. It has a small garden. ⓐ Dijver 5 🕿 050 33 60 69 🕸 www.dyver.be 🕐 12.00–14.00, 18.30–21.00 Fri–Tues

Den Gouden Harynck ££–£££ 🕬 This 17th-century building used to be a fish shop of the same name. Serves modern, innovative cuisine. ⓐ Groeninge 25 🕿 050 33 76 37 🕸 www.dengoudenharynck.be 🕐 12.00–14.00, 19.00–21.30 Tues–Fri, 19.00–22.30 Sat

Kardinaalshof ££–£££ 🕮 Smart gastronomic restaurant in a 19th-century house, specialising in fish and seafood. ⓐ Sint-Salvatorskerkhof 14 🕿 050 34 16 91 🕸 www.kardinaalshof.be 🕐 12.00–14.00, 19.00–21.30 Thur–Mon, 19.00–21.30 Tues (closed 2 weeks in July)

Patrick Devos ££–£££ 🕯 Inside this historic building with a superb Art Nouveau interior, Patrick Devos offers inventive gastronomic cuisine including a vegetarian menu. ⓐ Zilverstraat 41 🕿 050 33 55 66 🕸 www.patrickdevos.be 🕐 12.00–13.30, 19.00–21.00 Mon–Fri, 19.00–21.00 Sat

BARS & CLUBS

B-In The bar in this trendy restaurant (see page 87) buzzes until the early hours with a DJ and fantastic sound system. ⓐ Zonnekemeers 🕿 050 31 13 00 🕸 www.b-in.be 🕐 18.30–03.00 daily

't Brugs Beertje One of the best beer pubs in Bruges, offering around 300 brands of beer along with advice on what to drink. Open until late at the weekend. ⓐ Kemelstraat 5, off Steenstraat

🔺 *The traditional Maria van Bourgondië restaurant*

📞 050 33 03 51 🌐 www.brugsbeertje.be 🕐 16.00–01.00 Mon, Tues
& Thur, 16.00–02.00 Fri–Sun

Cafedraal Enjoy the medieval ambience with a drink at the bar.
There is also a restaurant here. ⓐ Zilverstraat 38 📞 050 34 08 45
🌐 www.cafedraal.be 🕐 11.30–23.00 daily

World Café The Top A fun place to be at weekends, with good music
and a friendly atmosphere. ⓐ Sint-Salvatorskerkhof 5 🕐 21.00–late
Tues–Sat, 22.00–late Sun (closed Wed, Nov–Apr)

Northeast of Markt

The area northeast of Markt tends to be more peaceful than the south, which can get crowded with visitors. It is an attractive area to walk through, with quiet canals, pocket-sized squares, notable churches and a handful of small museums. The St Anna district, once the poorer part of town and almost entirely residential, is a particularly lovely spot for a stroll. There are few shops, bars or restaurants there. Another good way to see the district is from a boat on the canal, as canal trips will take you along Sint-Annarei (St Anna Canal) for part of the way. The sunset along the canals in this area is beautiful.

Information about many of the sights and cultural attractions in the area can be found on ⓦ www.brugge.be

SIGHTS & ATTRACTIONS

Choco-Story

A delight for chocoholics and an excruciating temptation for slimmers, this private museum is popular with both children and adults. It tells the complete story of chocolate, starting with exhibits relating to its origins in the Maya and Aztec civilisations, following on with displays about the development of the chocolate trade and how chocolate is processed. There is a feature on Belgian chocolate, a short film to watch and a chocolate-making demonstration. By the time you reach the shop, there's no way you'll be able to resist the temptation to treat yourself. Don't miss the fabulous giant 120-kg (264-lb) Easter egg. ❸ Wijnzakstraat 2, Sint-Jansplein ① 050 61 22 27 ⓦ www.choco-story.be ⓛ 10.00–17.00 (closed 2 weeks in Jan, call for exact dates) ❶ Admission charge

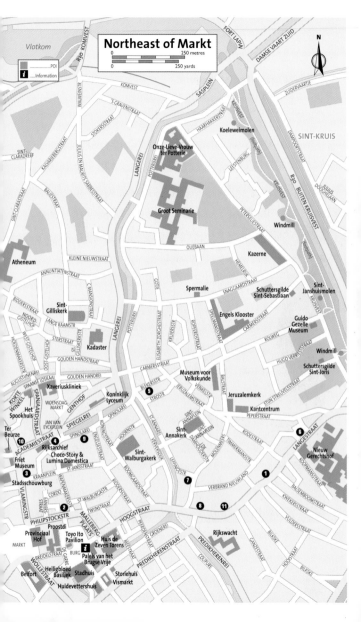

Vlotkom

R30 KOMVEST

0   250 metres
0   250 yards

POI
i Information

FORT LAPW

DAMSE VAART ZUID

N

SASPLEIN

ZUIDERVAARTJE

WALWINSTR

KOMVEST

'S GRAVENSTRAAT

STOKERSSTRAAT

HAARLIJKERSTRAAT

KRUISVEST

DAMPOORTSTRAAT

SINT-KRUIS

JULIUS EN MAURITS SABBESTRAAT

SINT-CLARADREEF

KALVERMEERKSTRAAT

BALESTRAAT

LANGEREI

POTTERIEI

LEESTENBURG

Koeleweimolen

Onze-Lieve-Vrouw
ter Potterie

HOENSTR

R30 BUITEN KRUISVEST

JULIUS DOOGHLAAN

KLEINE NIEUWSTRAAT

ANNUNTIATENSTRAAT

Atheneum

Groot Seminarie

OUDEBAAN

PETERSELESTRAAT

Windmill

C MANSIONSTR

BIDDERSSTRAAT

NOORD-GISTELHOF

WEST-GISTELHOF

HOEFIJZERSTRAAT

AUGUSTIJNENREI

Sint-
Gilliskerk

LANGE RAAMSTR

JAN VAN EYCKPLEIN

SPANJAARDSTRAAT

STERSTRAAT

GOUDEN HANDSTR

GILLISKERKSTR

JOH OSTRA

Kadaster

LANGEREI

POTTERIEI

CARMERSSTRAAT

ELISABETH ZORGHESTRAAT

KRUIESTR

SNAGGAARDSTRAAT

HEMELRIJK

Kazerne

Spermalie

Schuttersgilde
Sint-Sebastiaan

SPEELMANSSTRAAT

Engels Klooster

CARMERSSTRAAT

Sint-
Janshuismolen

Guido
Gezelle
Museum

HUGO VERRIESTSTRAAT

ROLWEG

Windmill

Schuttersgilde
Sint-Joris

GOUDEN HANDREI

GOUDEN HANDREI

Xaveriuskliniek

WOENSDAG MARKT

Koninklijk
Lyceum

Museum voor
Volkskunde

JERUZALEMSTR

FENNELSTR

STIJN STREUVELSTRAAT

BALSTRAAT

Jeruzalemkerk

Kantcentrum

PEPERSTRAAT

RODESTRAAT

KORTE
WINKEL

SPANJAARDSTRAAT

SPANJAARDSTR

SPINOLAREI

GENTHOF

JAN VAN
EYCKPLEIN

SPIEGELREI

SPINOLAREI

HOORNSTR

SINT-ANNAPLEIN

SINT ANNAREI

Het
Spookhuis

WDENSDAG
MARKT

SPIEGELREI

SINT-
ANNAKERK

LANGESTRAAT

Ter
Beurze

ACADEMIESTRAAT

KONINGSTRAAT

ENGELSESTRAAT

Sint-
Annakerk

SINT-ANNAPLEIN
SINT-
ANNAREI

TIMMERMANSSTR

Nieuw
Gerechtshof

KOORNMANSSTRAAT

10 Rijksarchief

4 Choco-Story &
Lumina Domestica

5

6

Friet
Museum
3

Stadsschouwburg

WAPENMAKERSSTR

SPAANPLEIN

ST-JANSSTRAAT

Sint-
Walburgakerk

BOOMGAARDSTR

LEFFINGESTR

1

7

VERBRAND NIEUWLAND

BALSEMBOOMSTRAAT

VLAMINGSTR

EIERMARKT

GELD-
MUNT
STRAAT

2

ST-WALBURGSTR

TWIJNSTRAAT

HOOGSTRAAT

VERVERSDIJK

GROENEREI

KWEKERSTRAAT

VLAMINGSTR

PHILIPSTOCKSTR

MALLEBERG
PLAATS

8

11

PREDIKHERENSTRAAT

BILSEK

HOOGPORT

Provinciaal
Hof

Proostdi

Toyo Ito
Pavilion

i

Huis de
Zeven Torens

Palais van het
Brugse Vrije

PREDIKHERENREI

COUPURE

Rijkswacht

PREDIKHERENREI

BILSEK

MARKT

BREIDELSTRAAT

DE CARRE

BURG

Belfort

Heiligbloed
Basiliek

WOLLE-
STRAAT

Stadhuis

Huidevettershuis

Storiehuis

Vismarkt

Engels Klooster (English Convent)

This large, domed building gets its name from the English Catholics who fled to the Spanish Netherlands in the 16th century. The refugees included nuns, who founded this establishment in 1629. The interior is essentially Baroque, dating from the 18th century. There are still nuns living here to this day.

⬤ *The 15th-century Jeruzalemkerk is still owned by descendants of its founder*

The exiled British King Charles II, who lived in Bruges from 1656 to 1659 before his restoration to the English throne, used to pray here and it later became a boarding school for English Catholic girls.

The convent isn't officially open to the public, but visitors are often allowed in at specified times. Check with the tourist office for details. ⓐ Carmersstraat 85 ⓣ 050 33 24 24 ⓛ 14.00–15.30, 16.15–17.15 Mon, Tues & Thur–Sat

Friet Museum (Belgian Fries Museum)

The Belgian love affair with the chip is legendary, and this museum celebrates it – from the origins of the tuber to its golden glory in the deep-fat fryer. You can also buy what are supposedly the best fries in Bruges at the end of your visit. ⓐ Vlamingstraat 33 ⓣ 050 34 01 50 ⓦ www.freitmuseum.be ⓛ 10.00–17.00 daily (closed mid-Jan); last admission 16.15 ⓘ Admission charge

Jeruzalemkerk (Jerusalem Church)

The Byzantine style of the Jerusalem Church makes it unique in Bruges. It was built by the Adornes (also known as Adorno) family of Genoa in the 15th century following a pilgrimage to Jerusalem. It is still owned by descendants of the family.

Part of the unusual interior is based on the Holy Sepulchre in Jerusalem. There are skulls on the altarpiece, symbolising Golgotha, and a black marble tomb containing the heart of Anselm Adornes. Adornes was murdered in Scotland in 1483, a grisly fact symbolised by the sword hilt emerging from the tomb. The 16th-century stained-glass windows tell the family's history.

The admission charge includes entry to the Lace Centre next door (see page 95). ⓐ Peperstraat 3 ⓣ 050 33 00 72 ⓛ 10.00–17.00 Mon–Sat ⓘ Admission charge

AN AFTERNOON STROLL

Start from Markt and walk along Vlamingstraat, passing the impressive Stadsschouwburg (City Theatre, see page 31), built in 1868 in neoclassical style. A little further along, you will come to the Friet Museum, and then to the carefully restored **Ter Beurze** house (❷ Vlamingstraat 35), the site of the world's first stock exchange in the 14th century. The van der Beurse family that owned it gave their name to the term *bourse* that is used for many of the world's stock exchanges today.

Next to the Ter Beurze house, the bookshop (no. 37) is housed in the former Venetian merchants' lodge. At the beginning of Academiestraat (no. 1) is the fashionable De Florentijnen restaurant (see page 102), previously the Florentine merchants' lodge. Spanjaardstraat, which leads off Academiestraat, was where Spanish traders once lived.

Continuing along Academiestraat, you will reach Jan van Eyckplein, a lovely, cobbled square with benches on the Spiegelrei Canal. The statue of the great Flemish painter Jan van Eyck was erected here in the 19th century.

Keep walking along Spiegelrei and you will come across the sites of more foreign merchants' lodges, including the 15th-century English lodge (no. 15). Further along the canal off Langerei is **Sint-Gilliskerk** (🕐 10.00–12.00, 14.00–17.00 Mon–Sat, 14.00–17.00 Sun, Apr–Sept), the church where Hans Memling is buried.

Walk back along the canal and cross the bridge at Genthof over to the St Anna district for a stroll among the small cottages with stained-glass windows. You can take a more direct route back to Markt via Hoogstraat and the Burg.

🔺 *Bruges's City Theatre*

Kantcentrum (Lace Centre)

In sharp contrast to the adjacent Jerusalem Church is the Lace Centre, housed in a row of almshouses. There are some outstanding examples of old handmade lace used both in the home and as clothing. Aim to go for the lacemaking demonstration from 14.00 in the Adornes family's former house. The admission charge includes entry to the Jerusalem Church (see page 93). Note that there are plans to move the centre to Balstraat 14 in 2012 or 2013; check with the tourist office. ❸ Peperstraat 3a ☎ 050 33 00 72 🌐 www.kantcentrum.com 🕐 10.00–17.00 Mon–Sat ❶ Admission charge

Onze-Lieve-Vrouw ter Potterie (Our Lady of the Pottery)

The hospital of Our Lady of the Pottery, run by monks and nuns, was founded in 1276. The church was added in the 14th century and renovated

▲ *The Bonne Chiere windmill*

in fancy Baroque style in the 17th century. It contains a statue of the Virgin and Child – venerated by some as miraculous – and some fine 17th-century tapestries. Some of the old hospital wards house an interesting collection of art, religious objects, items from the hospital and other exhibits.

Many of the hospital buildings have been renovated and today function as a retirement home. ❸ Potterierei 79 ❶ 050 44 87 11 🕐 09.30–12.30, 13.30–17.00 Tues–Sun ❶ Admission charge

Sint-Annakerk (St Anna Church)

A key landmark in the district with its slender spire, the parish church of St Anna has a charm that few other churches in Bruges

WINDMILLS

Windmills began to appear in Europe, particularly in the Netherlands and England, late in the 10th century. The idea was allegedly brought to Europe from the Middle East. Early European windmills were used for grinding grain. Later, their power was harnessed by engineers wanting to drain the marshy land found in low countries such as Belgium, Luxembourg and the Netherlands. In Bruges, many windmills were used to control the water flow in canals.

Between the 13th and 19th centuries, the city's outer ramparts (Kruisvest) boasted over twenty windmills. Only four remain today, two of which are open to the public and in working order. The Sint-Janshuismolen windmill, still in its original position, dates from 1770. The Koeleweimolen has been moved but is now open for visiting in summer. Both mills were originally used for grinding grain.

The Kruisvest itself, running alongside the canal, makes a great spot for a stroll with good views over the surrounding area. Look out for the massive old city gates of Kruisport near the Sint-Janshuismolen windmill, built in 1403. ❸ Kruisvest ⏱ Sint-Janshuismolen: 09.30–12.30, 13.30–17.00 Tues–Sun (May–Aug); Koeleweimolen: 09.30–12.30, 13.30–17.00 Tues–Sun (July & Aug) ℹ Admission charge

can match. Although originally finished in 1497, it was destroyed by arson in 1591 during the Wars of Religion. The interior dates from the 17th and 18th centuries, untouched by the neo-Gothic revival in the city. *The Last Judgement* over the entrance, by Hendrik Herregouts,

is the biggest painting in Bruges. ⓐ Sint-Annaplein ⓛ 10.00–12.00, 14.00–17.00 Mon–Sat, 14.00–17.00 Sun (Apr–Sept)

Sint-Walburgakerk (St Walburga's Church)

One of the hidden gems of Bruges, this light, peaceful, uplifting church was built by the Jesuits in 1619–43. With a black-and-white marble interior and an impressive organ, the church is generally much less ornate than you might expect of a Baroque building. It forms an interesting contrast in a city with so many Gothic and neo-Gothic buildings. Atmospheric music often plays in the background, even when there is no service. ⓐ Sint-Maartensplein, corner of Boomgaardstraat, Koningstraat & Hoornstraat ⓛ 10.00–12.00, 14.00–17.00 Mon–Sat, 14.00–17.00 Sun (Apr–Sept)

CULTURE

Guido Gezelle Museum

Guido Gezelle (1830–99) was one of Flanders's best-known poets, and the brick house in which he was born, with its large, pleasing garden, is now a museum dedicated to him and his work. Gezelle, a major figure in Dutch literature, was also a priest. His proud use of Dutch, when educated Belgium was dominated by French speakers, has made him something of a Flemish hero. The house will also give you a good impression of what life was like in 19th-century Bruges. The museum was recently modernised and reorganised around themes such as religion, nature and tradition.

The admission charge also gives entry to the Folklore Museum (see opposite). ⓐ Rolweg 64 ⓛ 09.30–12.30, 13.30–17.00 Tues–Sun ⓘ Admission charge

⬥ *The Folklore Museum evokes the atmosphere of bygone days*

Museum voor Volkskunde (Folklore Museum)

This fascinating museum, housed in a terrace of 17th-century almshouses, focuses on traditional local crafts and shops. There are displays of leatherwork and hat-making as well as the reconstructed interiors of a sweet shop and a pharmacy. The exhibits are vivid and interesting, and there are regular demonstrations of the crafts. The sweet-making demonstration (🕐 12.00–16.00 Thur) is a great treat for children. The museum also boasts a pleasant courtyard and café.

The admission charge also gives entry to the Guido Gezelle Museum (see opposite) and one of the windmills (see page 97).

📍 Balstraat 43 🕐 09.30–17.00 Tues–Sun ❶ Admission charge

Museum (see opposite) and one of the windmills (see page 97).

RETAIL THERAPY

Shopping isn't the main attraction of this area, but there are some interesting places to browse along Hoogstraat, Vlamingstraat, Academiestraat and Langestraat.

't Apostelientje Home-made quality lace. ⓐ Balstraat 11 ⓣ 050 33 78 60 ⓛ 10.00–18.00 Mon–Sat

Bacchus Cornelius Sells over 400 types of Belgian beer. The same family owns the chocolate and sweet shop next door, one of Bruges's oldest. ⓐ Academiestraat 17 ⓣ 050 34 53 38 ⓛ 10.00–18.30 Mon & Wed–Sat

Au Bonheur des Dames Antiques and decoration shop. ⓐ Hoogstraat 38 ⓣ 050 33 63 63 ⓦ www.desdames.be ⓛ 10.30–18.00 Tues–Sat

Joaquim & Jofre Exclusive women's fashions. ⓐ Vlamingstraat 7 ⓛ 11.00–18.00 Mon, 10.00–18.00 Tues–Sat

TAKING A BREAK

Frituur 't Bootje £ ❶ One of Bruges's best places to eat chips, this place also offers stews, kebabs and cold dishes. ⓐ Langestraat 91 ⓣ 050 34 20 76 ⓛ 11.30–14.00, 17.00–24.00 Sun, Mon, Wed & Thur, 17.00–02.00 Fri & Sat

De Lotus £ ❷ A charming organic vegetarian restaurant, open for lunch only, offering good-value set menus. ⓐ Wapenmakersstraat 5 ⓣ 050 33 10 78 ⓛ 11.45–14.00 Mon–Sat

Servaas Van Mullem £ ❸ A lovely patisserie opposite the
Stadsschouwburg, where you can read the paper at your leisure.
ⓐ Vlamingstraat 56 ❶ 050 33 05 15 ⓛ 07.30–18.00 daily

Jan van Eyck Tearoom £–££ ❹ A friendly tearoom and restaurant
in a pretty little square. ⓐ Jan van Eyckplein 12 ❶ 050 67 74 17
ⓛ Tearoom: 15.00–17.45 Thur–Tues (also open summer am);
restaurant: 12.00–14.30, 18.00–21.30 Thur–Tues (closed Sun pm)

Vlissinghe £–££ ❺ An inn since 1515, this popular place with
a garden serves hard and soft drinks, ice creams and snacks.
ⓐ Blekersstraat 2 ❶ 050 34 37 37 ⓦ www.cafevlissinghe.be
ⓛ 11.00–24.00 Wed–Sat, 11.00–19.00 Sun (Feb–Sept)

AFTER DARK

Although fairly quiet at night, some of Bruges's best restaurants are
in the area. The liveliest street is Langestraat and the canal makes
for a relaxing stroll.

RESTAURANTS

Sacre Coeur £–££ ❻ Relaxed bistro with a mixture of local and
international dishes and a young clientele. The bar inside is open
later. ⓐ Langestraat 137 ❶ 050 34 10 93 ⓛ 12.00–14.00, 18.00–24.00
daily (last food orders 22.00)

Relais Ravestein ££ ❼ The restaurant has two chefs; one prepares
simple traditional dishes with a contemporary twist and the other
specialises in Italian and fusion food. There is a seafood bar in the
summer and a terrace overlooking St Anna Canal. The bar is open for

drinks 11.00–late. ⓐ Molenmeers 11 ⓣ 050 47 69 47 ⓦ www.relais
ravestein.be ⓛ 12.00–15.00, 18.00–23.00 daily (kitchen closes 21.30)

Rock Fort ££ ❽ Popular new restaurant with a fresh, simple décor,
serving creative but affordable dishes. ⓐ Langestraat 15 ⓣ 050 33 41 13
ⓦ www.rock-fort.be ⓛ 12.00–14.00, 18.30–23.00 Mon–Fri

Spinola ££ ❾ Atmospheric upmarket restaurant offering high-
quality seasonal food including game and seafood. ⓐ Spinolarei 1
ⓣ 050 34 17 85 ⓦ www.spinola.be ⓛ 19.00–21.00 Mon, 12.00–13.30,
19.00–21.00 Tues–Sat (closed end Jan & June)

De Florentijnen £££ ❿ Chic restaurant serving Italian-influenced
modern dishes. Expect sharp, knowledgeable service and an impressive
wine list. ⓐ Academiestraat 1 ⓣ 050 67 75 33 ⓦ www.deflorentijnen.be
ⓛ 12.00–14.30, 19.00–22.30 Tues–Sat

De Karmeliet £££ ⓫ Renowned restaurant boasting three Michelin
stars, elegantly housed in a mansion with a garden. Formal atmosphere
and dress: jacket and tie for men are compulsory. ⓐ Langestraat 19
ⓣ 050 33 82 59 ⓦ www.dekarmeliet.be ⓛ 12.00–14.00, 19.00–22.00
Tues–Sat

BAR

Bar Salon Trendy tapas bar run by the owners of the Rock Fort
restaurant next door (see above). Good for a pre-dinner drink.
ⓐ Langestraat 17 ⓣ 050 33 41 13 ⓛ 11.00–23.00 Mon–Fri

▶ *The attractive city of Ghent*

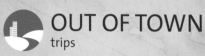

OUT OF TOWN
trips

Damme

The picturesque little village of Damme is named after the dam on the Zwin creek which allowed inhabitants to build up a formidable shipping cargo industry (see feature, page 108). Now the centre of an agricultural area, it's the perfect day-trip destination from Bruges. The place is popular, with over a million visitors flocking here each year to relax in the excellent restaurants and stroll through the quaint streets or along the canal. There is a windmill and a 15th-century herring market in the centre, as well as several shops.

One of the most pleasant things to do in the area, if you have a car or, even better, a bicycle, is visit the local villages such as Oostkerke, Vivenkapelle, Moerkerke and Lapscheure (near the border with the Netherlands). This will give you a real feel for the Flemish countryside and village life.

Information about many of the sights and cultural attractions in Damme can be found at the **tourist office**. ⓐ Jacob van Maerlanstraat 3 ⓣ 050 28 86 10 ⓦ www.toerismedamme.be ⓛ 09.00–12.00, 13.00–18.00 Mon–Fri, 10.00–12.00, 14.00–18.00 Sat & Sun (mid-Apr–mid-Oct); 09.00–12.00, 13.00–17.00 Mon–Fri, 14.00–17.00 Sat & Sun (mid-Oct–mid-Apr)

GETTING THERE

Damme is only 7 km (4½ miles) from Bruges and if you are feeling energetic it makes a great walk along the Bruges–Damme Canal. Set off from the Dampoort gate, near the northernmost windmill on the Kruisvest. You can also ride a bicycle along the canal path, or book a guided bike ride from Bruges covering the countryside around Damme with Quasimundo (see page 32).

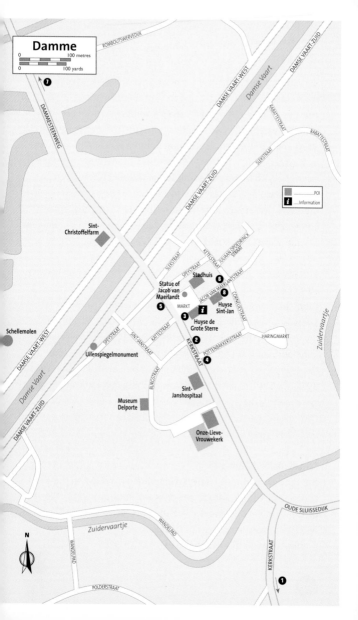

Damme

0 ——————— 100 metres
0 ——————— 100 yards

ROMBOUTSWERVEDIJK

DAMSE VAART-WEST

Damse Vaart

DAMSE VAART-ZUID

DAMMESTEENWEG

KARATESTRAAT

RABATESTRAAT

SLEKSTRAAT

POI

i ....Information

Sint-Christoffelfarm

SLEKSTRAAT

SPEYSTRAAT

KETELSTRAAT

JULIAAN OPDEDRINCK STRAAT

Stadhuis

JACOB VAN MAERLANTSTRAAT

Statue of Jacob van Maerlandt

❺

MARKT

JACOB VAN MAERLANTSTRAAT

CORNELISTRAAT

❻

❽

Huyse Sint-Jan

Schellemolen

DAMSE VAART-WEST

SPEYSTRAAT

SINT-JANSSTRAAT

KATTESTRAAT

i

❸

Huyse de Grote Sterre

❷

HARINGMARKT

Zuidervaartje

Uilenspiegelmonument

KERKSTRAAT

POTTENBAKKERSSTRAAT

❹

DAMSE VAART-ZUID

Damse Vaart

BURGSTRAAT

Sint-Janshospitaal

Museum Delporte

Onze-Lieve-Vrouwekerk

OUDE SLUISEDIJK

Zuidervaartje

WANDELPAD

WANDELPAD

KERKSTRAAT

N

❶

POLDERSTRAAT

❼

Damme is around a 10–15-minute drive along the road running parallel to the canal, with a taxi costing approximately €20–25 each way. Bus 43 leaves from Markt and the railway station every two hours between Easter and September, more frequently in the afternoon. The last return bus from Damme leaves at 18.09.

An interesting way to visit Damme is by canal boat. A one-way canal trip with **Lamme Goedzak Steam Wheeler** (🅰 Noorweegse Kaai 31 ☎ 050 28 86 10 🕒 Departures: 10.00, 12.00, 14.00, 16.00, 18.00 (Apr–mid-Oct) 🚊 Bus: 4, 799) lasts 35 minutes and will give you a different perspective on the countryside you pass through. Bicycles are now allowed on board.

SIGHTS & ATTRACTIONS

Onze-Lieve-Vrouwekerk (Church of Our Lady)

The oldest part of this imposing Gothic edifice – the section between the tower and the church – was erected in 1225. The church was modified in the 18th century, when the original nave, aisles and transept partially collapsed, but Damme's former wealth was severely diminished by this point and it was never restored to its former glory. You can climb the 43-m (141-ft) tower for some excellent views of Damme and the surrounding countryside. 🅰 Kerkstraat 🕒 14.00–17.00 Sat–Thur (Easter & May–Sept) 🛈 Admission charge

Schellemolen (Windmill)

You can visit Damme's nearest windmill, built in 1867 on the site of others dating back to the Middle Ages. There is an oil mill inside. 🅰 Damse Vaart West 🕒 09.30–12.30, 13.00–18.00 Sat, Sun & public holidays (Apr–Sept); as part of a guided tour booked through Damme tourist office at other times

● *Sint-Janshospitaal is both a home for the elderly and a museum*

Sint-Janshospitaal (St John's Hospital)

Dating from 1249, this attractive complex still functions as a hospital but is currently used mainly as a retirement home. It also contains a Baroque chapel and a museum of religious objects, ceramics, furniture and paintings. However, the building will cease to be a hospital from 2014, and its future is uncertain at the time of writing. ⓐ Kerkstraat 33 ❶ 050 46 10 80 Ⓦ www.ocmw-damme.be ⏱ 14.00–18.00 Mon & Fri, 11.00–12.00, 14.00–18.00 Tues–Thur, Sat & Sun (Easter–Sept) ❶ Admission charge

MINIATURE CITY

Damme, despite having only 700 inhabitants, is officially a city. Its surprising status derives from the vital role it had in the past as landing stage for large vessels offloading cargo to be transported up the canals on smaller boats and barges. At the height of its activity it was incredibly wealthy and, as well as the 300 types of goods that were regularly landed, the city had the special right to import Bordeaux wine and Swedish herrings. Charles the Bold, the last Duke of Burgundy and ruler of Flanders, even married Margaret of York, sister of Edward IV of England, in the city in 1468.

The silting up of the Zwin estuary in the 16th century put an end to Damme's cargo industry, and for a while both Bruges and Damme became backwaters. The Damse Vaart Canal now connects the two cities, but the only boats that put in here now carry tourists.

Stadhuis (Town Hall)

This notable Gothic building on the main square, with its sturdy and heavily augmented façade, was originally built in 1464 on the site of the old market hall. The exterior was restored in the 19th century. Two of the stone figures on the far right of the façade are of Charles the Bold and Margaret of York. The clock tower, which dominates the village, dates from 1459. In front of the Stadhuis is a 19th-century statue of Jacob van Maerlant (1235–93), a renowned Flemish poet and Damme resident.

The building is usually closed to the public but can be entered by arrangement with the tourist office. ❷ Markt

● *The attractive clock tower of the Stadhuis dates back to 1459*

RETAIL THERAPY

There are the usual souvenir shops in Damme but very few others, except for those serving the daily needs of the local population, and a surprising number of bookshops.

Galerie Indigo An art gallery also selling unique gifts and quality clothing. ② Kerkstraat 15 ① 050 37 03 31 ⓦ www.indigoartgallery.be ① 11.00–13.00, 14.00–18.00 Mon, Tues & Fri, 14.00–18.00 Thur, 11.00–18.00 Sat & Sun

Tijl en Nele A small souvenir and snack shop selling local specialities, including beer. ② Jacob van Maerlantstraat 2 ① 050 35 71 92 ① 09.30–18.30 Sat–Thur (Apr–Nov); 09.30–18.30 Sat–Wed (Dec–Apr)

TAKING A BREAK

De Ijshoeve £ ❶ Stop off at 'The Ice-Cream Farm' on the outskirts of Damme and sample a delicious home-made ice cream or one of the

BOOKS
Damme has established itself as something of a literary hotspot, with several bookshops opening up here since the late 1990s. Most of them sell second-hand books, some in English. The shops are open daily May–September, but only at weekends during the rest of the year. There is a book market in the main square every second Sunday of the month, which transfers to the Town Hall during the winter.

🔺 *The market square viewed from the top of the Gothic Stadhuis*

other mouthwatering sweet snacks made from fresh farm produce. ⓐ Oude Damse Weg 2a ① 050 37 39 87 Ⓦ www.deijshoeve.be ① 13.30–18.00 Tues–Fri & Sun, 10.30–12.00, 13.30–18.00 Sat (Apr–Oct)

Tante Marie £ ② A bright, modern tearoom with many outside tables serving salads, snacks, home-made pastries and ice creams to eat in or take away. ⓐ Kerkstraat 38 ① 050 35 45 03 Ⓦ www.tante marie.be ① 10.00–21.00 daily (summer); 10.00–19.00 daily (winter)

Eetcafé de Spieghel £–££ ❸ Brasserie in a 16th-century merchant's house on the main square, with tables outside. Snacks available out of dining hours. ⓐ Jacob van Maerlantstraat 1 ⓣ 050 37 11 30 ⓦ www.despieghel.be ⓛ 11.00–24.00 Wed–Mon, summer (kitchen closes 22.00); 11.30–15.00, 18.00–22.00 Wed–Sun, winter

AFTER DARK

RESTAURANTS

Le Bonheur ££ ❹ The newest of Damme's fine restaurants. The menu is short but interesting, and is dominated by impressive fish and seafood. ⓐ Kerkstraat 26 ⓣ 050 85 84 78 ⓦ www.le-bonheur.be ⓛ 12.00–14.00, 18.30–21.00 Wed–Sun

De Drie Zilveren Kannen ££ ❺ Situated on the main square and serving quality, traditional cuisine. Specialities include fresh lobster, rib-eye steak and *paling in het groen* (eel in chervil sauce). This 15th-century gabled restaurant boasts a smart, candlelit interior. ⓐ Markt 9 ⓣ 050 35 56 77 ⓛ 11.30–15.00, 17.30–22.00 Tues–Sun

De Lieve ££ ❻ One of Damme's oldest restaurants, rustic in style but serving high-quality gastronomic food and excellent wines. ⓐ Jacob van Maerlantstraat 10 ⓣ 050 35 66 30 ⓦ www.delieve.com ⓛ 12.00–14.30 Mon, 12.00–14.00, 18.00–21.30 Wed–Sun

Siphon ££ ❼ One of the best-known restaurants in the country, serving Belgian food and game in season. A little way out of town, but worth seeking out. ⓐ Damse Vaart-Oost 1, Oostkerke ⓣ 050 62 02 02 ⓦ www.siphon.be ⓛ 11.00–15.00, 17.00–late Sat–Wed

● *Eetcafé de Spieghel offers a traditional, homely atmosphere*

De Zuidkant ££ ❶ High-quality contemporary food in this relaxed restaurant with an open kitchen. ⓐ Jacob van Maerlantstraat 6 ❶ 050 37 16 76 🕐 19.00–21.00 Fri, 12.00–14.00, 19.00–21.00 Sat–Mon

BARS
De Smisse A lively café-bar attracting a young crowd. Good background music, a wide selection of beers and an outside terrace. ⓐ Kerkstraat 6 ❶ 050 35 12 46 ⓦ www.desmisse.com 🕐 09.00–late Tues–Sun

ACCOMMODATION

De Speye £ This two-star hotel is the only one in the centre, small but pleasant and quiet. Offers bike hire. ⓐ Damse Vaart-Zuid 5–6 ❶ 050 54 85 42 ⓦ www.hoteldespeye.be

Ghent

On the junction of two rivers, the Leie (Lys) and the Scheldt (Schelde), Ghent ('Gent' in Dutch, 'Gand' in French) is an important port as well as being capital of the East Flanders province. With its cobbled, pedestrianised streets and compact centre, it looks superficially similar to Bruges. But don't be fooled – unlike Bruges it has several local heavy industries, including car production, and is a vibrant university town full of young, ambitious people.

The old façades of many buildings give way to ultra-modern interiors, completely rebuilt rather than restored in their original style as in Bruges. An excellent example of this dizzying architecture is, appropriately, the Design Museum (see page 121). You can also pop into the Miljoenenkwartier area behind the railway station to see a surprising number of fine Art Nouveau and Art Deco buildings.

All the main sights are located in the city centre, which consists basically of four linked squares: Korenmarkt, Sint-Baafsplein, Groentenmarkt and Vrijdagmarkt. The area is being progressively pedestrianised and it is easy and pleasant to walk around. You can also take a **horse and carriage ride** (ⓐ Sint-Baafsplein ⓣ 09 227 62 46 ⓛ 10.00–18.00 daily (Mar–Nov); tours last 30 mins) or a **guided canal boat trip** (ⓐ Various landing stages: Kraanlei, Korenlei, Graslei or the Groentenmarkt bridge ⓛ 10.00–18.00 daily (Mar–Nov); tours last 40 or 90 mins) with commentary in various languages. **Tourist office** ⓐ Botermarkt 17a (in Belfort crypt) ⓣ 09 266 56 60 ⓦ www.visitgent.be ⓛ 09.30–18.30 daily (summer); 09.30–16.30 daily (winter)

Note that the tourist office is likely to move to the old fish market (Oude Vismijn ⓐ Sint-Veerleplein 5, near the castle) some time during 2012. The new office will have interactive data displays.

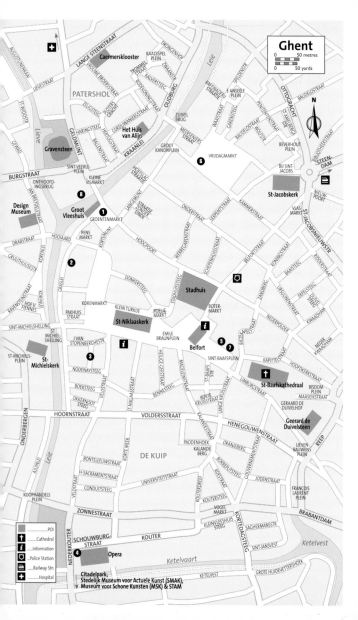

GETTING THERE

Trains from Bruges to Gent Sint-Pieters station leave every half-hour and take roughly 20–25 minutes to reach Ghent. You can take tram 1 from the station to Korenmarkt in the city centre, a 15-minute ride away. There is also a taxi rank at the station, and a new bike-hire area is being built.

Ghent is 40 km (25 miles) from Bruges by car along the E40. Parking in the city centre, however, can be difficult and using public transport is a cheaper and better option.

SIGHTS & ATTRACTIONS

If you plan to visit several of the main attractions, it's well worth buying a three-day **Museum Pass**. This is available from the tourist office or museums, and includes free travel on buses and trams. Tram 1 will take you close to most of Ghent's museums.

Belfort

The 91-m (298-ft) belfry dominates the skyline of Ghent and can be seen from all over the city. It is topped by a gilded copper weathervane in the shape of a dragon. It was once the city's watchtower; the bells were used to warn the citizens of danger from enemies and to announce major events. Construction first started in early 1314, but the tower has had many makeovers through the years, particularly in the 19th century. The current dragon dates from just 1980.

The Belfort has six floors, with a small museum on the first and second, the bells on the third, the clock mechanism on the fifth, and excellent views of the city from the sixth. You can take a lift as

🔺 *The Belfort was once Ghent's watchtower*

PARTY CITY

Ghent plays host to several festivals during the year,
particularly in the summer. The best and liveliest is the ten-
day **De Gentse Feesten** (Ghent Festivities Ⓦ www.gentse
feesten.be) in late July. It's actually four festivals in one –
a colourful extravaganza of jazz, dance, street-theatre and
puppet shows. During the ten days, numerous open-air and
free music events take place around the city.

The important **Flanders International Film Festival**
(Ⓦ www.filmfestival.be) is held in Ghent during October.
Some 250 feature and short films are shown over the 12 days
as part of a competition focused on the impact of music on film.

Ghent also has a new **Light Festival**, when the city is
illuminated by artists and designers. The festival is held every
two years, with the next one in January 2014.

far as the fourth floor. ➌ Sint-Baafsplein Ⓛ 10.00–18.00 daily (mid-
Mar–mid-Nov) ❶ Admission charge

Gravensteen (Castle of the Counts)

This imposing edifice was built in 1180 by Philip of Alsace, Count
of Flanders, and has been heavily restored since then. The castle
boasts displays of various weapons as well as a small museum of
instruments of torture. You can also see the dungeons. There are
some great views of the city from the battlements. ➌ Sint-
Veerleplein ❶ 09 225 93 06 Ⓛ 09.00–18.00 daily (summer);
09.00–17.00 daily (winter); last admission 1 hour before closing
❶ Admission charge

◆ *The imposing Gravensteen has been heavily restored*

◓ The Design Museum's exhibits include Art Nouveau and Art Deco pieces

CULTURE

Design Museum

This superb museum opened in 1992 in the 18th-century Hotel de Coninck. The first few rooms are deceptively decorated in a traditional style, displaying older furniture and other artefacts. The heart of the museum, however, is firmly contemporary, consisting of bold, bright spaces displaying Art Nouveau and Art Deco exhibits as well as objects by designers such as Phillipe Starck, Ron Arad and Jean Nouvel. There are regular temporary exhibitions. ⓐ Jan Breydelstraat 5 ⓣ 09 267 99 99 ⓦ www.designmuseumgent.be ⓛ 10.00–18.00 Tues–Sun ⓘ Admission charge

Museum voor Schone Kunsten (Museum of Fine Arts)

The recently renovated Museum of Fine Arts (often referred to as MSK) boasts 40 rooms containing one of the finest collections of paintings in Belgium. Exhibits range from medieval Flemish paintings to 20th-century works, many of them acquired in the 18th century from old churches and other religious institutions. Included are works by Brueghel, Hals, Tintoretto, Rubens, Renoir, van Dyck and Kokoschka. There are regular temporary exhibitions. ⓐ Citadelpark ⓣ 09 240 07 00 ⓦ www.mskgent.be ⓛ 10.00–18.00 Tues–Sun ⓘ Admission charge

Sint-Baafskathedraal (Cathedral of St Bavo)

Named after St Bavo, the local 7th-century saint, this cathedral was originally founded in the 10th century, or possibly earlier, as the first parish church of Ghent. It was known as St John's and, after several enlargements, became a cathedral in 1561. The predominantly Gothic exterior contains no fewer than 22 chapels and several fabulous works of art, including Rubens's *The Conversion of St Bavo*. The 12th-century

Romanesque crypt – one of the biggest in Belgium – is the oldest existing part. It also contains several fine Flemish paintings and some impressive frescoes dating from the 15th and 16th centuries.

The highlight is the huge *Adoration of the Mystic Lamb*, also known as *The Ghent Altarpiece*, painted by brothers Jan and Hubert van Eyck in 1432. Housed in a separate chapel (note the different opening times), the famous work has been repeatedly stolen – most recently by the Nazis – and recovered. One panel, stolen in 1934, is still missing. Although the altarpiece has been in the cathedral for many years, there are plans to move it elsewhere for security and conservation reasons. ⓐ Sint-Baafsplein ⓘ 09 225 16 26 ⓦ www.sintbaafskathedraal-gent.be ⓛ Cathedral: 08.30–18.00 (summer); 08.30–17.00 (winter), closed to visitors during services; *Adoration of the Mystic Lamb*: 09.30–17.00 Mon–Sat, 13.00–17.00 Sun (summer); 10.30–16.00 Mon–Sat, 13.00–16.00 Sun (winter) ⓘ Admission charge

STAM (Ghent City Museum)

Ghent's newest museum (opened in late 2010) is housed in a superbly modernised old abbey and convent, parts of which date to the 14th century. The history of the city is explored through impressive and imaginative displays, many interactive or multimedia, which will appeal to children. Special exhibitions deal with city-living in general. It also has an attractive café and picnic areas. One of the best ways to get there is by boat. ⓐ Bijlokesite, Godshuizenlaan 2 ⓘ 09 267 14 00 ⓦ www.stamgent.be ⓛ 10.00–18.00 Tues–Sun ⓘ Admission charge

Stedelijk Museum voor Actuele Kunst (City Museum of Contemporary Art)

One of the finest museums of modern art in Belgium, the Stedelijk Museum (SMAK) opened in 1975. The museum displays works by

David Hockney, Francis Bacon and Andy Warhol, as well as by Belgian artists such as Magritte. Major special exhibitions are displayed on the ground floor. ❸ Citadelpark ❶ 09 221 17 03 ❿ www.smak.be ❻ 10.00–18.00 Tues–Sun ❶ Admission charge

RETAIL THERAPY

For smart shops and international chains, head for Veldstraat, south of Korenmarkt, or Langemunt, just off Groentenmarkt. Burgstraat is good for antiques and bric-a-brac, while Hoogpoort and Bennesteeg are the best streets for fashion and accessories. There are small boutiques, food and speciality shops scattered around the old city. Note that many smaller shops don't take credit cards.

Markets are colourful and popular in Ghent. Try browsing the **flower market** (❸ Kouter ❻ 07.00–13.00 daily), **flea market** (❸ Bij Sint-Jacobs ❻ 08.00–13.00 Fri–Sun) or **food market** (❸ St-Michielsplein ❻ 07.30–13.00 Sun). Vrijdagmarkt is filled with stalls selling new goods on Fridays and Saturdays, and on Sunday mornings the same square transforms into a feathery bird market.

The Fallen Angels Two linked and thoroughly eccentric shops selling old toys, religious memorabilia, bric-a-brac and old postcards. ❸ Jan Breydelstraat 29–31 ❶ 09 223 94 15 ❻ 13.00–18.00 Mon & Wed–Sat

Het Oorcussen One of the best women's clothes shops in town, with clothes by leading Belgian designers. ❸ Vrijdagmarkt 7 ❶ 09 233 07 65 ❻ 13.30–18.00 Mon, 10.30–18.00 Tues–Sat

Temmerman A charmingly old-fashioned confectionery shop selling sweets, chocolates and biscuits, including the local speciality *cuberdon*

(conical sweets made from raspberry syrup and gum arabic).
🅐 Kraanlei 79 ❶ 09 224 00 41 🕒 10.00–18.00 Mon–Sat

Tierenteyn-Verlent This beautiful shop in a 16th-century building
sells hot home-made mustard and a good selection of herbs, spices,
oils and vinegars. 🅐 Groentenmarkt 3 ❶ 09 225 83 36 🕒 10.00–
18.00 Tues–Sat

TAKING A BREAK

The centre of Ghent is packed with stylish restaurants and cafés,
many of them by the waterside. You can buy picnics in the
delicatessens or markets, and relax to eat them by a canal or in the
leafy Citadelpark. There is also a popular chip kiosk in Vrijdagmarkt.

🔺 *The waterfront is good for a stroll and a coffee*

Groot Vleeshuis £ ❶ On the site of the covered 15th-century meat market, this restaurant and delicatessen serves excellent East Flemish snacks. Outside tables. ⓐ Groentenmarkt 7 ❶ 09 223 23 24 ⓦ www.grootvleeshuis.be ⓛ 10.00–18.00 daily

AFTER DARK

Ghent boasts several concert halls, theatres, art centres, cinemas and an opera house (with resident opera company) so there's no shortage of evening entertainment. Much of the centre of Ghent is floodlit at night and, unlike Bruges, the city has a dynamic nightlife. Some of the hippest places for music and dancing are outside the centre.

RESTAURANTS

Belga Queen £–££ ❷ One of Belgium's most famous brasseries, serving top-quality food in a converted 13th-century grain storehouse by the Leie river. Go for a set-menu lunch or afternoon tea. ⓐ Graslei 10 ❶ 09 280 01 00 ⓦ www.belgaqueen.be ⓛ 12.00–14.30, 19.00–23.00 Mon–Wed, 12.00–14.30, 19.00–24.00 Thur–Sat, 12.00–14.30, 18.30–23.00 Sun

Brasserie Pakhuis £–££ ❸ A fashionable place in an old warehouse, serving French and Italian cuisine featuring excellent seafood. ⓐ Schuurkenstraat 4, off Nodenaysteeg ❶ 09 223 55 55 ⓦ www.pakhuis.be ⓛ 11.30–01.00 Sun–Thur, 11.30–02.00 Fri & Sat

Café Théatre £–££ ❹ Modern, split-level bar and restaurant with dark brown walls and a relaxed atmosphere. ⓐ Schouwburgstraat 5 ❶ 09 265 05 50 ⓦ www.cafetheatre.be ⓛ Restaurant: 12.00–14.15,

19.00–23.00 Mon–Thur, 12.00–14.15, 19.00–24.00 Fri, 19.00–24.00 Sat, 12.00–14.00, 19.00–23.00 Sun; bar: 10.00–late daily

De Foyer £–££ ❺ Beautiful original interior wood panelling in the Flemish Theatre's restaurant, with a large balcony overlooking the square and excellent international cuisine. ⓐ Sint-Baafsplein 17 ❶ 09 234 13 54 ⓦ www.foyerntgent.be ⓛ Kitchen: 12.00–14.00, 18.30–22.00 Wed–Sun; bar: 10.30–late Wed–Sun

Keizershof £–££ ❻ Well-established Belgian restaurant in a handsomely restored building. ⓐ Vrijdagmarkt 47 ❶ 09 223 44 46 ⓦ www.keizershof.net ⓛ 12.00–14.00, 18.00–22.00 Tues–Sat

't Vosken £–££ ❼ A popular, traditional brasserie close to the cathedral. ⓐ Sint-Baafsplein 19 ❶ 09 225 73 61 ⓛ 11.00–24.00 daily

Bord'eau ££ ❽ Large and extremely stylish new restaurant and bar with a riverside terrace, housed in the old fish market. The mainly Belgian food is simple but excellent, with very good-value lunch and dinner menus. ⓐ Sint-Veerleplein 5 ❶ 09 223 20 00 ⓦ www.bordeau.be ⓛ Kitchen: 12.00–14.30, 19.00–22.00 Mon–Sat (closes 22.30 Fri & Sat), 12.00–15.00 Sun; bar: 12.00–01.00 Mon–Sat, 11.00–18.00 Sun

BARS
Dulle Griet An atmospheric bar offering 250 types of beer and snacks. ⓐ Vrijdagmarkt 50 ❶ 09 224 24 55 ⓛ 16.30–01.00 Mon, 12.00–01.00 Tues–Sat, 12.00–19.30 Sun

Mélangoest This bar offers tasty tapas and meals as well as drinks. ⓐ Schouwburgstraat 18 ❶ 09 324 47 19 ⓛ 10.00–01.00 Tues–Sat

ACCOMMODATION

Ghent has accommodation to suit all pockets and tastes. Book early if you are planning to visit for the Ghent Festivities in late July. See Ⓦ www.visitgent.be for more hotel listings.

Ibis Gent Centrum Opera £ Good-value chain hotel with pleasant rooms. ⓐ Nederkouter 24–26 ⓣ 09 225 07 07 Ⓦ www.ibis hotel.com

Monasterium £ Simple, brightly decorated rooms in an old monastery. Rooms in the adjacent guesthouse are not en-suite. ⓐ Oude Houtlei 56 ⓣ 09 269 22 10 Ⓦ www.monasterium.be

Ghent River Hotel ££ Modern hotel in two old buildings on the Leie river. ⓐ Waaistraat 5 ⓣ 09 266 10 10 Ⓦ www.ghent-river-hotel.be

Hotel de Flandre ££ A stylish, comfortable B&B in a converted 19th-century inn. ⓐ Poel 1–2 ⓣ 09 266 06 00 Ⓦ www.hotelde flandre.be

Hotel Verhaegen ££ Tiny but stylish four-room hotel in an old mansion. ⓐ Oude Houtlei 110 ⓣ 09 265 07 60 Ⓦ www.hotelverhaegen.be

Marriott ££–£££ Central luxury hotel on one of the main canals. ⓐ Drabstraat, corner of Korenlei ⓣ 09 233 93 93 Ⓦ www.marriott ghent.be

NH Gent Belfort ££–£££ Smart and comfortable with excellent facilities. ⓐ Hoogpoort 63 ⓣ 09 233 33 31 Ⓦ www.nh-hotels.com

Ypres & World War I battlefields

Ypres ('Ieper' in Danish, or 'Wipers' as British Tommies called it) was the site of some of World War I's bloodiest battles. Some 500,000 soldiers died in the area, half of them from Britain and the Commonwealth, and many more thousands were wounded. It is a powerful experience to see the incredible number of graves that surround the town, spread over 170 cemeteries. Among those buried here are British, Belgian, French and American soldiers, commemorated by the Menin Gate and the In Flanders Fields Museum.

Most visitors – many of them descendants of those who fought or died here – come to see the battlefields and war graves, learn about World War I, and remember those who lost their lives. Ypres is overwhelmed on Remembrance Day (11 Nov). The town is attractive in itself, retaining some of the grandeur of its previously wealthy status as a major player in the cloth trade. From its heyday in the 13th century, however, when it had 40,000 inhabitants and an active industry, it suffered economic decline and remained quietly in the background until the World War I bombardment started. After 40 years of painstaking restoration work, the town's mainstay is tourism. People are extremely friendly and English is spoken almost everywhere. Major events are planned for the centenary of World War I.

As well as being a useful source of visitor information, the **tourist office** also has a stylish shop selling books, postcards and souvenirs. ⓐ Lakenhal, Grote Markt 34 ⓣ 057 23 92 20 ⓦ www.visitypres.be ⓛ 09.00–18.00 Mon–Sat, 10.00–18.00 Sun & public holidays (Apr–mid-Nov); 09.00–17.00 Mon–Fri, 10.00–17.00 Sat, Sun & holidays (mid-Nov–Mar)

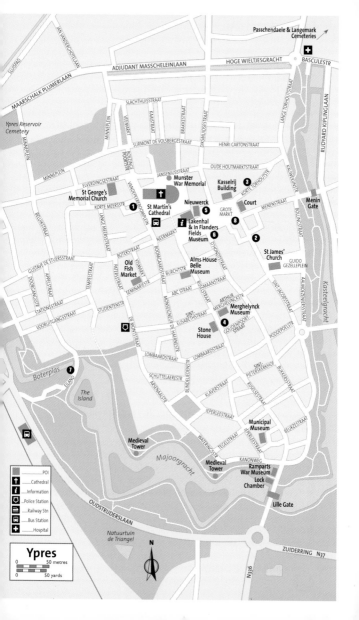

Ypres

Passchendaele & Langemark Cemeteries

BASCULESTR

ADJUDANT MASSCHELEINLAAN   HOGE WIELTJESGRACHT

MAARSCHALK PLUMERLAAN

SLUISPAD

JAN VANDERPECHTLAAN

Ypres Reservoir
Cemetery

MINNEPLEIN

SLACHTHUISSTRAAT

KAASTRAAT

BAKKERSSTRAAT

DIKSMUIDSESTRAAT

SURMONT DE VOLSBERGESTRAAT

HENRI CARTONSTRAAT

VEEMARKT

MINNESTRAAT

ELVERDINGSESTRAAT

JANSENIUSSTRAAT

OUDE HOUTMARKTSTRAAT

Munster
War Memorial

Kasselrij
Building ❸

St George's
Memorial Church

KORTE MEERSSTR

LANG MEERSSTRAAT

VANDERPEERBOOMPLEIN

BISCHOP POORTPLEIN

BELLEWAARDE

GUSTAVE DE STUERSSTRAAT

DOORGANGSSTR

APPELSTRAAT

STATIONSSTRAAT

VOORUITGANGSSTRAAT

TEMPELSTRAAT

PATTEESSTRAAT

BOTERSTRAAT

VISMARKT

BOOMGAARDSTRAAT

SEMINARIESTR

STUDENTENSTR

DE MONTSTRAAT

STONE
HOUSE

LOMBAARDSTRAAT

SCHUTTELAERESTR

ARSENAALSTR

BLINDELIEDENSTR

Boterplas

ELAND

The
Island

Majoorgracht

Medieval
Tower

Medieval
Tower

OUDSTRIJDERSLAAN

Natuurtuin
de Triangel

N336

❶ St Martin's
Cathedral

Nieuwerck

❺

Lakenhal
& In Flanders
Fields Museum ❻

GROTE
MARKT

Court

❾

❷

KORTE TORHOUTSTR

LANGE TORHOUTSTR

MENENSTRAAT

BOLLINGSTRAAT

St James'
Church

GUIDO
GEZELLEPLEIN

SINT JACOBSSTRAAT

AALMOEZENIERSSTRAAT

RIJSELSTRAAT

Menin
Gate

KALINEHUISSTR

RUDYARD KIPLINGLAAN

Kasteelgracht

Old
Fish
Market

BURCHTSTR

ABC STRAAT

RIJSELMAANSTRAAT

SINT-ELISABETHSTRAAT

Alms House
Belle
Museum

Merghelynck
Museum ❹

Stone
House

GOUDENPOORT

ARTHUR
MERGHELYNCKSTR

SINT-
PIETERKERKHOF

KLAVERSTRAAT

IEPERLEESTRAAT

WATENWEG

TEGELSTRAAT

Municipal
Museum

BEKELEESTRAAT

D'HONDTSTRAAT

BUDELSTRAAT

BLIKSEMSTRAAT

PODDEPOELSTR

BUKESTRAAT

BEURZESTRAAT

KANONWEG

Ramparts
War Museum

Lock
Chamber

Lille Gate

ZUIDERRING N37

N336

Legend

▪ POI
✝ Cathedral
ℹ Information
Ⓢ Police Station
🚇 Railway Stn
🚌 Bus Station
✚ Hospital

0 ———— 50 metres
0 ———— 50 yards

N

❼

GETTING THERE

Regular trains from Bruges to Ypres take around two hours, changing at Kortrijk. The station is a 10-minute walk from the centre of town. Driving takes an hour or more on the A17, E403 and A19, and you can often find parking in the market square (unless the Saturday market is on) or behind the Cloth Hall. Parking may be difficult at peak times over summer and on Remembrance Day.

Quasimodo (Ⓦ www.quasimodo.be) is one of the best tour companies offering full-day mini-coach trips to Ypres and the Flanders battlefields, with lunch, drinks and museum entry included. The tours are in English. ⬤ Tues, Thur & Sun (Feb, Mar, Nov & Dec); Tues–Sun (Apr–Oct)

SIGHTS & ATTRACTIONS

Battlefields & cemeteries

The best way to visit the battlefields and cemeteries is in the company of a knowledgeable guide, who can explain the history behind the moving experience. Some of the best guided visits are with the **Flanders Battlefield Tour** (Ⓦ www.ypres-fbt.com), **Salient Tours** (Ⓦ www.salienttours.com) and **Speedy's Battlefield Tours**

> **LOCATING A GRAVE**
> If you want to locate a particular grave in a cemetery, contact the helpful **Commonwealth War Graves Commission** in Ypres (📞 057 223 636 Ⓦ www.cwgc.org). Many minibus tours will allow you to visit individual graves on advance request.

(www.sbt-ypers.be), which can also transport you straight back to Bruges. **Over the Top Tours** (www.overthetoptours.be) is run by three British professional historians. Others include **The Original Over the Top Tours** (www.overthetoptours-ypres.be), **Frontline Tours** (www.frontline-tours.com) and **Lest We Forget Tours** (http://lestweforget.vpweb.be). The last two offer more personalised visits.

🔺 *Remembering those who died in World War I at Ypres*

◆ *The 13th-century Lakenhal at Ypres*

You will need a car or a bicycle to visit the battlefields by yourself. Bicycles can be hired from Ypres railway station and the Ambrosia Hotel (see page 140), and the tourist office can provide you with special route maps. The cemetery at Passchendaele (Passendale) is particularly moving, and the German cemetery at Langemark – where 45,000 German soldiers are buried – is also worth visiting for its very different design and atmosphere.

Grote Markt (Main Square)

Take a look around the town's main square to appreciate some of the grandeur of this formerly wealthy cloth town. Aside from the huge and impressive Lakenhal (Cloth Hall, see below), it is worth admiring the Kasselrij building, the former Town Hall in the middle of the square, with its beautifully carved medallions above the windows representing the Seven Deadly Sins. The current Town Hall, the **Nieuwerck** (🕙 08.30–11.45 Mon–Fri), boasts a grand council chamber. It was originally built in 1619 but destroyed in World War I and rebuilt in 1962.

Just behind the Cloth Hall is the Gothic **St Martin's Cathedral** (🕙 09.00–17.00 Mon–Fri & Sun 09.00–16.00 Sat, closed to visitors during services & 12.00–14.00), again completely rebuilt after World War I. Nearby is **St George's Memorial Church** (🕙 09.30–16.30 or dusk; closed to visitors during services), an Anglican church designed by London architect Sir Reginald Blomfield in 1928–9 to commemorate the war dead.

Lakenhal (Lakenhalle, Cloth Hall)

The Cloth Hall was the largest non-religious building in Europe when it was built in the 13th century, when Ypres's lucrative cloth industry was at its height. It was the main cloth and wool market in

⏺ The names of almost 55,000 missing soldiers are engraved on the Menin Gate

CAT-THROWING

Stuffed toy cats are thrown off the belfry tower of the Cloth Hall by a jester as part of the triennial *Kattenstoet* (Cat Festival) on the second Sunday in May. The colourful festival commemorates the bizarre medieval practice of throwing real cats from the tower. There are many theories as to how this tradition came about – some more fantastical than others. Many think that it is because cats were believed to be linked to witchcraft; others that it is because there were too many of the creatures roaming the streets in those days. Revellers at the festival dress as cats or witches, or in historical costume, and the cat-throwing is followed by a ceremonial mock witch-burning in the main square.

the area and, with its 70-m (230-ft) belfry tower topped by a gilded dragon, is a testament to the city's prestige at the time. The Hall was almost completely destroyed by artillery fire in World War I and it took 34 years of painfully slow building work to restore it to its former glory. The belfry has been a UNESCO World Heritage Site since 1999. The huge warehouse on the upper floors now houses the In Flanders Fields Museum (see page 137). ❷ Grote Markt 34

Menin Gate

One of Ypres's most impressive sights is the Menin Gate by the city's ramparts. Designed by Sir Reginald Blomfield, also the architect of St George's Memorial Church, this poignant and very dignified memorial has the names of almost 55,000 missing British and Commonwealth soldiers engraved on its walls.

The Last Post is sounded every evening at 20.00 from under the gate's imposing archway. This traditional salute has been repeated every day since 1928, honouring those soldiers of the former British Empire who fought and died in Ypres during World War I.
Ⓦ www.lastpost.be

◢ One of the atmospheric displays at the In Flanders Fields Museum

CULTURE

In Flanders Fields Museum

This superb, modern museum housed on the first floor of the Cloth Hall brilliantly evokes the atmosphere and history of World War I with moving displays and the latest interactive techniques. The museum closed to be renovated and enlarged in late 2011, and is due to reopen in June 2012. Last entry is one hour before closing.
ⓐ Grote Markt 34 ☎ 057 23 92 20 ⓦ www.inflandersfields.be

WAR POETRY

The greatest suffering can sometimes inspire the greatest creativity. From the profusion of war poetry that appeared unexpectedly from the battlefields of World War I, three names stand out: McCrae, Owen and Sassoon.

The Canadian John McCrae (1872–1918) served as a field surgeon during the Second Battle of Ypres in 1915. His most famous poem, *In Flanders Fields*, was inspired by the death of his close friend Alexis Helmer during the battle. With its heart-wrenching pride in death it rapidly became one of the most popular poems of the war. The poppies referred to in the first line: 'In Flanders Fields the poppies blow' are now the symbol of Remembrance Day.

Killed in action just a week before the war ended, the bitter, tortured verses of the British poet Wilfred Owen (1893–1918) take on an even more ironic twist. His *Dulce et Decorum Est* juxtaposes the patriotic Roman sentiment *dulce et decorum est pro patria mori* ('it is sweet and fitting to die for your

country') with nightmarish imagery of young soldiers actually fighting and dying in the trenches.

Owen was heavily influenced by his friend and mentor Siegfried Sassoon (1886–1967), whom he had met while recuperating at the Craiglockhart War Hospital in Edinburgh. Sassoon's satirical anti-war verses rail against wartime propaganda with horrifying descriptions of death, rotting corpses, filth and misery. He is perhaps best known for his public letter *A Soldier's Declaration*, a brave 'act of wilful defiance of military authority' in refusing to return to service, and a condemnation of the 'callous complacency' with which those safely at home treated the lives of soldiers on duty.

🕐 10.00–18.00 daily (Apr–mid-Nov); 10.00–17.00 Tues–Sun (mid-Nov–Mar) ❶ Admission charge

RETAIL THERAPY

Ypres is not the place for a shopping trip, but the small centre contains several chocolate and beer shops. There are also some bookshops catering to those with an interest in World War I.

TAKING A BREAK

The best cafés and bars are near Grote Markt and the Menin Gate.

't Leetvermaak £ ❶ Friendly and welcoming owners. Serves traditional Flemish cuisine complemented by a selection of more

exotic dishes. ⓐ Korte Meersstraat 2 ⓣ 057 21 63 85 ⓛ 18.00–24.00 Tues & Sat, 11.30–13.30, 18.00–23.00 Wed–Fri & Sun

Old Bill £ ❷ Lively Irish pub that often has live folk and rock music. ⓐ Sint-Jacobsstraat 10 ⓣ 057 21 55 20 ⓛ 16.00–01.00 Tues–Sun

The Times £ ❸ Cosy pub but no food served. ⓐ Korte Torhoutstraat 7 ⓣ 0473 66 45 81 ⓦ www.the-times-ypres.be ⓛ 11.00–14.00, 16.30–late Fri–Wed

Het Zilveren Hoofd £ ❹ Offering 16 different authentic Belgian beers. ⓐ Rijselstraat 49 ⓣ 057 36 03 67 ⓛ 11.00–late Tues–Sat; food: 11.30–14.00, 18.30–22.00 Tues–Sat

AFTER DARK

RESTAURANTS
There are plenty of excellent restaurants in Ypres serving good-quality food to suit all tastes and pockets. During busy periods, such as around Remembrance Day, they can get busy, so do make sure you book in advance.

In 't Klein Stadhuis £ ❺ The 'Little Town Hall', next door to the real one, is inviting and friendly, serving decent food in a warm atmosphere. There are free live music events on Tuesday evenings during the summer months. ⓐ Grote Markt 32 ⓣ 057 21 55 42 ⓦ www.kleinstadhuis.be ⓛ 09.00–23.00 Mon–Fri, 09.00–24.00 Sat

Old Tom ££ ❻ Cosy hotel restaurant specialising in fish, seafood and game when in season. Also offers interesting culinary theme

nights. ⓐ Grote Markt 8 ⓣ 057 20 15 41 ⓦ www.oldtom.be ⓛ 12.00–14.30, 18.00–21.30 Thur–Tues

Pacific Eiland ££ ❼ Regional food next to the ramparts and the water. Also has a bistro and tearoom, and a terrace in the summer. ⓐ Eiland 2 ⓣ 057 20 05 28 ⓦ www.pacificeiland.be ⓛ 10.00–19.00 Mon, 10.00–22.00 Wed–Sun

Regina ££ ❽ A hotel restaurant with a warm welcome and high-quality cooking. ⓐ Grote Markt 45 ⓣ 057 21 88 88 ⓦ www.hotelregina.be ⓛ 12.00–14.00, 18.30–21.30 Tues–Sat

ACCOMMODATION

Ambrosia Hotel £ A small, friendly hotel in the centre of Ypres. English breakfast is included. Bicycle rental is available at €10 per day. ⓐ D'Hondtstraat 54 ⓣ 057 36 63 66 ⓦ www.ambrosiahotel.be

Flanders Lodge £ An atmospheric wooden lodge, now part of the Best Western chain. ⓐ Albert Dehemlaan 19 ⓣ 057 21 70 00 ⓦ www.bestwestern.be

Ariane ££ A modern, central hotel with friendly staff, a five-minute walk from the main square. ⓐ Slachthuisstraat 58 ⓣ 057 21 82 18 ⓦ www.ariane.be

❶ *Canal-side road and footpath in Bruges*

PRACTICAL
information

Directory

GETTING THERE

By air

The closest international airport to Bruges is Brussels Airport (see page 48), which has regular flights to and from the UK with **British Airways** (Ⓦ www.ba.com), **Brussels Airlines** (Ⓦ www.brusselsairlines.com) and **bmi** (Ⓦ www.flybmi.com). **Aer Lingus** (Ⓦ www.aerlingus.ie) flies from Dublin. Most other major cities in the world also have connections to Brussels Airport, including direct flights with Delta, American Airlines and British Airways from New York, and with Air Canada, Delta, British Airways and Lufthansa from Toronto. **Ryanair** (Ⓦ www.ryanair.com) flies from Manchester, Glasgow Prestwick, Dublin and Shannon to Charleroi Airport, an hour away from Brussels. See page 48 for information on transferring to Bruges.

Many people are aware that air travel emits CO_2, which contributes to climate change. You may be interested in the possibility of lessening the environmental impact of your flight through the charity **Climate Care** (Ⓦ www.climatecare.org), which offsets your CO_2 by funding environmental projects around the world.

By rail

The easiest way to travel to Bruges is by train. There are up to ten Eurostar trains a day to Brussels from London St Pancras, Ebbsfleet International or Ashford International. On arrival at Brussels Midi/Zuid station you can change for a regular direct train to Bruges (trains leave around every 30 minutes). If you book your Eurostar ticket to 'Any Belgian Station' on the website, onward (and return) travel is included in your ticket at a reduced cost. Not only is this cheaper, but it's also

more convenient than buying a ticket in Brussels. Total journey time to Bruges is around three and a half hours.

Eurostar ☎ 08432 186 186 (UK) Ⓦ www.eurostar.com

By road

The cheapest way to reach Bruges is by coach, but it is also the slowest. **Eurolines** (Ⓦ www.eurolines.com) offers regular coach trips from London to Brussels Nord railway station, via Dover and Lille, with a journey time of around eight or nine hours. You can then take the train from Brussels Nord to Bruges.

It is not advisable to bring a car into Bruges as the centre is tiny and one-way streets make navigating difficult. Parking can be a problem, particularly at peak times, though several hotels have car parks. There is a ring-road encircling the city.

🔺 *Hop on and sit back for a tour of the city's delights*

By sea

The closest ferry port is Zeebrugge, which has regular connections with Hull and Rosyth. There are also services from Dover to Calais and from Ramsgate to Ostend. The Eurotunnel is another option. From Calais or Ostend, take the E40/A10 road to Bruges.

Eurolines Ⓦ www.eurolines.com

Eurotunnel Ⓦ www.eurotunnel.com

Norfolk Line Ferries Ⓦ www.norfolkline.com

P&O Ferries (Dover, Hull) Ⓦ www.poferries.com

Transeuropa Ferries (Ramsgate) Ⓦ www.transeuropaferries.com

ENTRY FORMALITIES

All visitors to Belgium require a valid passport or, for EU citizens, a national identity card. Citizens of the UK, Republic of Ireland, US, Canada, Australia and New Zealand do not require a visa for stays of up to three months. Citizens of other countries, or those wishing to stay longer than three months, may need a visa. See Ⓦ www.diplomatie.be or contact your embassy for more information.

Residents of the UK, Ireland and other EU countries may bring into Belgium possessions and goods for personal use, including a reasonable amount of tobacco and alcohol, provided they have been bought in the EU. Residents of non-EU countries, and EU residents arriving from a non-EU country, may bring in up to 400 cigarettes or 50 cigars or 50 g (2 oz) of tobacco, and 2 litres (three bottles) of wine or 1 litre (about 2 pints) of spirits and liqueurs.

MONEY

The euro (€) is the official currency in Belgium. Euros come in notes of €5, €10, €20, €50, €100, €200 and €500. Coins are in denominations of €1 and €2, and 1, 2, 5, 10, 20 and 50 cents. €1 = 100 cents.

ATM machines can be found at the airport, railway stations and in several locations around Bruges, including the main post office. They accept most British and international debit and credit cards.

There are a number of *Wissel* (bureaux de change) in Bruges, including at the tourist office. Try **Goffin Change** (ⓐ Steenstraat 2) or **Pillen R W J** (ⓐ Rozenhoedkaai 2). Banks will also change currency – remember to take your passport. Many hotels offer currency exchange but rates are often unfavourable; it's normally cheaper to use an ATM.

Traveller's cheques are not widely accepted in restaurants and shops, and you will need a passport or other photo ID in order to cash them. A better bet is to use a prepaid currency card such as those available from ⓦ www.fairfx.com or ⓦ www.caxtonfx.com

Credit cards are widely accepted in larger restaurants and shops but be aware that in smaller establishments, particularly in the surrounding villages, they are not. The most widely accepted credit cards are Visa, MasterCard and American Express.

HEALTH, SAFETY & CRIME

Medical facilities in Belgium are excellent but expensive. UK citizens are covered by EU reciprocal health schemes on production of a European Health Insurance Card (EHIC). See ⓦ www.ehic.org.uk for more information on obtaining a card. Remember that this will not cover all possible expenses, and only guarantees emergency treatment. Always make sure you have adequate travel insurance.

UK health and travel advice ⓦ www.fco.gov.uk/travel or ⓦ www.dh.gov.uk (click on 'EHIC & Information for travellers')
US health and travel advice ⓦ www.cdc.gov/travel or ⓦ www.healthfinder.com

Apotheek (pharmacies), indicated by a green cross sign, are plentiful around the city and have expert staff qualified to offer medical advice on minor ailments and to dispense a wide range of medicines. Many drugs that are widely available in the UK can only be bought at pharmacies in Belgium.

Tap water in Bruges is safe to drink and the standard of hygiene in restaurants and shops is very high.

Bruges is a safe place and the biggest danger, as in any popular city, is pickpocketing. Make sure that you keep your wallet hidden and your bag firmly zipped with the strap over your shoulder. Take particular care around the railway station and in crowded cafés, and keep your valuables locked in a hotel safe.

OPENING HOURS

Most shops are open 09.00–18.00 Monday to Saturday, although smaller establishments generally close at lunchtime. Food and tourist shops have longer opening hours and are often open on Sundays. The main markets (see page 25) are open 08.00–13.00.

Bank opening hours vary. Most are open 09.00 or 09.30–16.00 or 16.15 Monday to Friday, closing for an hour or two over lunch. There are some that remain open over lunch and close earlier in the afternoon. All banks are closed on public holidays.

Most of the main museums are open 09.30–17.00 Tuesday to Sunday, with last entry at 16.30. Museums are almost always closed on Mondays, except Easter and Whit Monday. Opening times of churches and private museums vary.

TOILETS

There are public toilets in the old market hall in the Belfort, in the Sint-Janshospitaal complex, at the railway station, in 't Zand Square

and in Bargplein, just south of Minnewaterpark. There is usually a small charge, but they are generally clean and well kept. All of the main museums have good toilet facilities. If you pop into a café or restaurant to use the toilets, it is polite to buy a drink there or at least to ask beforehand.

CHILDREN

Bruges is a child-friendly place – small, lively and easy to walk around – and children are welcome in all but the most formal restaurants. There are plenty of sweet shops and stalls selling chips, ice creams and waffles to keep them fed and happy. Children under 13 are allowed free entrance to municipal museums.

Supplies such as nappies and baby food are best bought from supermarkets. Pharmacies do sell them, but they tend to be expensive.

�delta *The lake in Bruges's Minnewaterpark*

There are no big supermarkets (and only a few small ones) in the city centre, so if possible bring adequate supplies with you, along with any regular medication.

There are few attractions specifically geared towards children in Bruges, but there are many that they will love. Older children will enjoy Choco-Story (see page 90), the Friet Museum (see page 93), the Archaeology Museum (see page 81), and the colourful Folklore Museum (see page 99) with its reconstructions and demonstrations.

A visit to the windmills (see page 97) is a treat for children of all ages, and a novelty horse-drawn carriage or canal boat ride will also excite them. If they need to burn off some energy, take them to the adventure playground at the Astridpark just south of Markt.

If you can time your visit to coincide with one of Bruges's festivals (see pages 8, 10 & 12), such as the Choco-Laté with its chocolate village and children's workshops, they'll have a holiday to remember.

COMMUNICATIONS
Internet
Many hotels now offer Internet and Wi-Fi access, but Internet cafés in the city centre are rather thin on the ground. Try:

Bauhaus Cybercafé ⓐ Langestraat 135 ⓦ www.bauhaus.be
Snuffel Backpacker Hostel Also offers free Wi-Fi connection.
ⓐ Ezelstraat 47–49 ⓣ 050 33 31 33 ⓦ www.snuffel.be
Teleboetiek ⓐ Corner of Langestraat & Predikherenstraat
ⓣ 050 61 67 69

Phone
Public telephones are fairly rare in the city centre. Some accept prepaid phonecards and some only take coins. You can buy a phonecard from the post office, railway stations and newsagents.

TELEPHONING BRUGES

The international code for Belgium is 32 and the area code for Bruges is 050. When dialling from inside Belgium – even when inside the area itself – dial the area code plus the telephone number. When dialling from abroad, dial either 00 (from the UK), 011 (from the US) or 0011 (from Australia), followed by the international code (32), followed by the area code without the first zero (50) plus the telephone number.

TELEPHONING ABROAD

To make an international call from Belgium dial 00, followed by your country code (UK 44; Republic of Ireland 353; USA and Canada 1; Australia 61; New Zealand 64; South Africa 27), followed by the area code (leaving out the first 0 if there is one) plus the telephone number.

Phone rates in hotels tend to be astronomical, particularly for international numbers. Do ask before calling. Mobile phone network coverage is generally good throughout Bruges and is probably the most convenient option for a short trip. Check with your mobile phone provider regarding coverage and tariffs.

Directory enquiries (English-speaking service) ℹ 1405

Post

The Belgian postal service is generally efficient and mail to the UK will normally take two or three days to arrive, a little longer to destinations outside Europe. You can buy stamps at the post office, newsagents and tobacconists. Postboxes are either the traditional

red pillar boxes or holes in the wall, marked with the word *Poste*.
Central Post Office ❸ Markt 5, near the Belfort 🕐 09.00–18.00
Mon–Fri, 09.00–15.00 Sat

ELECTRICITY

Electrical current in Belgium is 220V AC and plugs are the standard
European round two-pin ones. British appliances will need a simple
adaptor; these can be obtained in most UK electrical shops, or at the
Eurostar station or airport. You will also be able to find shops in
Bruges selling adaptors, although you might have difficulty in the
very centre. US and other equipment designed for 110V AC will
usually need a transformer.

TRAVELLERS WITH DISABILITIES

Cobbled streets, medieval buildings and crowded tourist areas do
not generally make life easy for travellers with disabilities. Access
is improving, however. The Eurostar and the train line from Brussels
to Bruges are now accessible for wheelchair users, with lifts to most
platforms, ramps for boarding the train, disabled toilets, and trained
staff available to help daily from 06.00 to 22.00.

Buses in Bruges commissioned since 2004 have step-free access
and wheelchair spaces as well as drivers trained to help passengers
with physical or visual impairments. Moreover, the city centre is
small, fairly flat and relatively easy to get around without the use of
public transport.

Museums, restaurants and hotels are gradually acquiring facilities
for disabled visitors, in particular those with mobility issues, and
the city looks set to become much more accessible in the future.
Currently, it is still always best to call and check in advance, being
clear about your needs.

Bruges tourist office (see below) will provide helpful information on the accessibility of individual places. The official access website (Ⓦ www.accessiblebruges.be) uses pictograms to illustrate the various facilities offered by establishments in the city.

Europe For All An excellent online information service offering plenty of advice for disabled travellers within Europe. Ⓦ www.europeforall.com

RADAR The principal UK forum and pressure group for people with disabilities. Ⓐ 12 City Forum, 250 City Road, London EC1V 8AF Ⓣ 020 7250 3222 Ⓦ www.radar.org.uk

SATH (Society for Accessible Travel & Hospitality) Advises US-based travellers with disabilities. Ⓐ 347 Fifth Ave, Suite 610, New York, NY 10016 Ⓣ 212 447 7284 Ⓦ www.sath.org

TOURIST INFORMATION

The main In&Uit Brugge tourist office, based in the Concertgebouw, also sells maps, guides, combined entrance tickets for museums and tickets to events in the city. There is an accommodation booking service and Internet access (see page 20).

USEFUL WEBSITES
Bruges tourist information Ⓦ www.brugge.be
Damme tourist information Ⓦ www.toerismedamme.be
Flanders tourist information Ⓦ www.visitflanders.co.uk
Ghent tourist information Ⓦ www.visitgent.be
Shopping in Bruges Ⓦ www.bruggebusiness.com
Ypres tourist information Ⓦ www.toerisme-ieper.be

⬤ *Enjoying the sun by the statue of Jan Breydel*

There is also a tourist information office at the railway station
🕐 09.30–12.30, 13.00–17.00 Tues–Sat

For listings information regarding events and festivals, pick up
a copy of the free monthly *Exit* magazine from the tourist office.
Ⓦ www.exit.be

BACKGROUND READING

A Portrait of Bruges by Georges-Henri Dumont & Vincent Mercx.
The secrets of Bruges are revealed in this bewitching, photo-filled
hardcover book illustrating the city's fascinating past.

A Tall Man in a Low Land by Harry Pearson. A highly entertaining,
witty and affectionate look at the country and culture through the
eyes of someone who has visited just about every nook and cranny
of Belgium.

Bruges: The City Behind the History by Roel Jacobs & Jan Vernieuwe.
A magnificent hardcover, photo-illustrated guide to the city.

The Fair Face of Flanders by Patricia Carson. Describes Flanders's own
individual character in an accurate and lively way from a historian's
point of view.

Flanders: A Cultural History by André de Vries. Explores the varied
landscapes of Flanders, both rural and urban, to reveal this region's
unique character.

FILMS

The 2008 black comedy *In Bruges*, starring Colin Farrell and Brendan
Gleeson as professional killers, was filmed in the city, which very
much co-stars.

Fred Zinnemann's 1959 film *The Nun's Story*, starring Audrey
Hepburn, was also partially shot in Bruges.

Emergencies

The following are emergency toll-free numbers:

All emergencies ℹ 112
Ambulance ℹ 100
Emergency doctor or dentist ℹ 100
Fire ℹ 100
Police ℹ 101

MEDICAL SERVICES

Hospitals are located at:

AZ Sint-Jan The main city hospital, with a *Spoedgevallen* (Accident & Emergency) department. ⓐ Ruddershove 10 ℹ 050 45 21 11; emergencies: 050 45 20 00 Ⓦ www.azbrugge.be

AZ Alma (Campus Sijsele) Small not-for-profit hospital. ⓐ Gentse Steenweg 132 ℹ 050 72 81 11; emergencies: 050 72 81 00

AZ Sint-Lucas Private hospital with A&E department. ⓐ Sint-Lucaslaan 29 ℹ 050 36 91 11 Ⓦ www.stlucas.be

Your hotel or the tourist office should advise you of the nearest English-speaking doctors in the area. If you need a doctor at the weekend (🕒 20.00 Fri–08.00 Mon), call ℹ 050 36 40 10

For information on out-of-hours pharmacies, check the door of a pharmacy or call ℹ 0900 10 500 (🕒 09.00–22.00 daily).

POLICE

If you are the victim of crime, go straight to the central police station to report it. You may need the documents you will receive for insurance purposes. Police (*politie*) are friendly, efficient and helpful, and often speak English.

Central Police Station ⓐ Hauwerstraat 3 ℹ 050 44 88 44

EMBASSIES & CONSULATES

Australia ⓐ Guimard Centre, Rue Guimard 6–8, Brussels
ⓣ 02 286 05 00 ⓦ www.belgium.embassy.gov.au
Canada ⓐ Avenue de Tervueren 2, Brussels ⓣ 02 741 06 11
ⓦ www.belgium.gc.ca
New Zealand ⓐ Square de Meeûs, 7th floor, Brussels ⓣ 02 512 10 40
ⓦ www.nzembassy.com/belgium
Republic of Ireland ⓐ Rue Wiertz 50, Brussels ⓣ 02 235 66 76
South Africa ⓐ Rue Montoyer 17–19, Brussels ⓣ 02 285 44 00
ⓦ www.southafrica.be
UK ⓐ Rue Arlon 85, Brussels ⓣ 02 287 62 11
ⓦ http://ukinbelgium.fco.gov.uk
USA ⓐ Boulevard du Régent 27, Brussels ⓣ 02 508 21 11
ⓦ http://usembassy.gov.be

ACKNOWLEDGEMENTS

Thomas Cook Publishing wishes to thank ANWER BATI, to whom the copyright belongs, for the photographs in this book, except for the following images:

AM/PM Bed & Breakfast/Kevin Van Volcem, page 38; Sébastien Barillot, page 23; Cel Fotografie Stad Brugge, pages 9, 13, 96 & 99; Dreamstime.com (Tom Davidson, page 35; Asta Plechaviciut, pages 40–41); Fotolia.com (Jerome Berquez, page 33; Jean-Jacques Cordier, page 5); iStockphoto.com (Flavia Bottazzini, page 30; Alison Cornford-Matheson, page 52; Franky De Meyer, page 7; Mike Morley, page 141; Govert Nieuwland, page 59; Joan Quevedo Fle, page 62; Stan Rippel, page 49; J Tan, page 86; Laurent Willen, page 71); Pandhotel/Jan Verlinde, page 37; D H Snover/ BigStockPhoto.com, page 47; Tourism Flanders, pages 76, 131, 147 & 152.

For CAMBRIDGE PUBLISHING MANAGEMENT LIMITED:
Project editor: Ed Robinson
Layout: Paul Queripel
Proofreaders: Tom Lee & Karolin Thomas

Send your thoughts to
books@thomascook.com

- Found a great bar, club, shop or must-see sight that we don't feature?
- Like to tip us off about any information that needs a little updating?
- Want to tell us what you love about this handy little guidebook and more importantly how we can make it even handier?

Then here's your chance to tell all! Send us ideas, discoveries and recommendations today and then look out for your valuable input in the next edition of this title.

Email the above address (stating the title) or write to: pocket guides Series Editor, Thomas Cook Publishing, PO Box 227, Coningsby Road, Peterborough PE3 8SB, UK.

WHAT'S IN YOUR GUIDEBOOK?

Independent authors Impartial up-to-date information from our travel experts who meticulously source local knowledge.

Experience Thomas Cook's 165 years in the travel industry and guidebook publishing enriches every word with expertise you can trust.

Travel know-how Thomas Cook has thousands of staff working around the globe, all living and breathing travel.

Editors Travel-publishing professionals, pulling everything together to craft a perfect blend of words, pictures, maps and design.

You, the traveller We deliver a practical, no-nonsense approach to information, geared to how you really use it.

The author would like to thank Anita Rampall, Aude Criqui, Anne De Meerleer, Freya Sackx, Jean-Pierre Drubbel, Bert Van Haecke, Tina Van Poucke, Lyn Vanhaecke and Cécile Buisset for their help.

Useful phrases

English	Dutch	Approx pronunciation
BASICS		
Yes	Ja	*Ya*
No	Nee	*Nay*
Please	Alstublieft	*Als-too-bleeft*
Thank you	Dank u wel	*Dank oo vel*
Hello	Dag/Hallo	*Dakh/Hallo*
Goodbye	Dag/Tot ziens	*Dakh/Tot zeens*
Excuse me	Pardon	*Par-don*
Sorry	Sorry	*Soree*
That's all right	Dat geeft niet, hoor	*Dat khayft neet, hor*
I don't speak any Dutch	Ik spreek geen Nederlands	*Ik sprayk khayn Nederlands*
Do you speak English?	Spreekt u Engels?	*Spraykt-oo Eng-els?*
Good morning	Goedemorgen	*Khooda-morkha*
Good afternoon	Goedemiddag	*Khooda-middakh*
Good evening	Goedenavond	*Khooda-afont*
Goodnight	Goedenacht	*Khooda-nakht*
My name is...	Ik heet...	*Ik hayt...*
NUMBERS		
One	Een	*Ayn*
Two	Twee	*Tway*
Three	Drie	*Dree*
Four	Vier	*Feer*
Five	Vijf	*Fayef*
Six	Zes	*Zess*
Seven	Zeven	*Zayfen*
Eight	Acht	*Akht*
Nine	Negen	*Naykhen*
Ten	Tien	*Teen*
Twenty	Twintig	*Twintikh*
Fifty	Vijftig	*Fayeftikh*
One hundred	Honderd	*Honderd*
SIGNS & NOTICES		
Airport	Vliegveld	*Fleekh-felt*
Railway Station	Trein Station	*Trayn Sta-syon*
Platform	Spoor/Perron	*Spoar/Perron*
Smoking/Non-smoking	Roken/Niet Roken	*Roh-keh/Neet Roh-keh*
Toilet	Toilet	*Twa-let*
Ladies/Gentlemen	Dames/Heren	*Daam-es/Heer-ren*
Bus	Bus	*Boos*